AF324757

Shifting Lives Media

Nashville ~ New York

Table of Contents

Acknowledgements

We want to thank our family for their steadfast support. Their encouragement was strength for us.

Thank you to all of our clients who taught us much about the connection from the Subconscious mind to the issues in their daily lives and encouraged us to bring this wonderful Method to the world.

Our special thanks to our son Michael for his endless hours of transcribing, Justin Vero for his research contributions, and Ben Dulaney for proof reading.

We thank our Divine Creator and the celestial navigation for love and direction during the writing of the book.

Perhaps the most valuable result of all education is the ability to make yourself do the thing you have to do, when it ought to be done, whether you like it or not.

~ Thomas Henry Huxley ~

Introduction

This book is divided into two parts.

Part One is stories drawn from actual testimonials about the work done at Shifting Lives involving our unique Shifting Lives Method.

Part Two is about the conscious mind and the subconscious mind. We will take an in depth look at the conflicting thoughts and beliefs that arise between these two aspects of mind. Our clients are often unaware of the differences in beliefs held in the conscious and subconscious mind. Also, a variety of daily practices will be discussed; with committed use of these methods you will achieve a higher level of personal development.

For those of you who have an understanding of the mind and the subconscious, we encourage you to begin with Part One. However, if you are uncertain of the actions performed by the subconscious, we encourage you to read Part Two first to gain an understanding of the universal laws governing mind-action.

In Part One, you will find several compelling examples about various aspects of life.

Relationships are extremely important to everyone. In our sessions, we have found among clients a prevalence of negative thought constructs like being afraid of love, having guilt when receiving love, and being unable to give love. We have also found "a fear of people loving me for my possessions and/or money," resulting in "only being lovable when I am poor or disabled."

There is a chapter about the heartaches of money and finances, which is also prevalent in many of our clients' lives today, and it additionally covers the personal side of this delicate subject.

You'll meet a musician who was down on his luck, and through our program, he found his muse and rebuilt his life. Now, he is at the top of the charts with more fame and fortune than he had ever imagined would be possible.

You'll meet a businessman who was a failure in at least five different enterprises. He discovered the common denominator in his difficulties was his own self. Using our method, he fixed his limitations, and he is now a very successful entrepreneur. His life has improved on both his business and personal levels.

You'll meet a woman who was physically injured over thirty years ago, and she discovered how this one incident had subconsciously paralyzed her life, profoundly crippling her mental choices.

These are just a few of the numerous examples you'll find in Part One.

Our work at Shifting Lives is based on the reality that *IT'S NOT THEM.*

It is never the person or appearance *out there* that is causing us difficulties or causing us to react in certain ways. It is what is within the self.

If there is only one thing that you take from this book, this is it.

IT'S NOT THEM!

It is NOT the government. It is NOT where you live. It is NOT where you went to high school. It is NOT your gender. It is nothing outside your-self.

It is all within ourselves and our perceptions and the filters we have created.

The themes of our lives are based on how we were raised and our modeling behaviors. They're also based on our beliefs, and our disbeliefs, and the component parts of self, which include our physical body, our emotional well-being, our mental health, our spiritual nature, our relationships, and our career/finances.

How do we make the all encompassing parts of ourselves the best we can possibly be?

This book will help you create a better version of yourself, and according to Albert Schweitzer, the best way to help the world at large is to improve ourselves.

We look for cycles, patterns, and experiences that keep repeating over and over in our lives because the common denominator when you see things reoccurring in your life is YOU.

We talk about the reactive mind versus the proactive mind.

The reactive mind is connected to an imaginary big red button that some people have on their chests that says "PUSH HERE" because their subconscious mind is trying to create a scenario where their button will be pushed.

One interesting fact about those buttons is that the more people push on them the more lively they become. With repeated stimulus, there is a building up of the responses to the point where sometimes all it takes is a word, a shrug, or a cutting of the eyes to cause someone to blow up and go totally berserk.

The truth is that seemingly "little" stimulus has been occurring over and over again for years, even decades, building and festering ready to explode.

The second aspect is the proactive self. Using our knowledge and our wisdom to understand that every scenario we encounter is a new and fresh opportunity, we can respond to it from a clean slate instead of reacting to it like we have in the past.

So, if oftentimes you find yourself in the slow line at the grocery check-out counter agitated and upset when you see ten people buzz by you in the other lanes while you are stuck behind the fumbling, bumbling person who needs a price check, can't find a credit card, and has a pen that doesn't write sending you over the edge into a complete melt-down, then this book is for you.

You will discover why this happens over and over again in your life and why you create these experiences repeatedly.

We also discuss the cooperative mind versus the competitive mind.

Part One consists of stories relating to the most common aspects of life revealing the thoughts, feelings, and emotions commonly experienced by so many people today.

Part Two is about the mind, the subconscious, and the many different methods you can practice to help bring yourself into a higher level of personal development.

This book will explain how the world, culture, our parents, modeling behavior, our teachers, and all the different people in our lives influence and shape us. By defining the difference in the orders of consciousness, we can identify what is troubling us.

We identify your issues, determine what to do about them, and offer solutions that you can practice on a daily basis.

If you are troubled by fears, doubts, worries, or concerns this book is for you. If there are cyclic patterns in your life, or you are seeing evidence of self-punishment showing up in your world, we offer help and guidance.

Here I Am. Now What?

Clarification of Terms

Due to the nature of our work, we often have to use words that define subconscious scenarios from the subconscious point of view. Sufficient language has not been created to fully express the way the subconscious mind reacts to our beliefs and the constructs it creates.

Some of the terminologies used in this book are not restricted to the dictionary definitions of the word.

We use words like control, abandoned, dread, and disgust, and each of these words may have a meaning slightly varied from the classic dictionary definition.

The subconscious has a unique filter that expresses itself through thought constructs, created scenarios, and events. Therefore, it reacts to certain words and phrases discovered by shifting lives over 20 years of exploration.

Statements in session are phrases that speak the language of the subconscious mind. We will denote these statements throughout the book by enclosing them in double quotes.

When we say that someone has a "fear of men", we don't mean that they consciously have a fear of men although they may. In fact, it's often quite the opposite. A lot of times they are very, very fond of men. Even, overly fond, but since they have a subconscious fear of men, their relationships with men seem to self-destruct for no apparent reason much to their chagrin.

*Nobody can make you feel
inferior without your consent.*

~ Eleanor Roosevelt ~

Chapter One

False Authority and Personal Power

My Prized Kitten

One day, a woman came into my clinic seeking help for a general vague feeling that had engulfed her life. She kept running into situations that keep happening to her over and over for no apparent reason.

In our work, we are always interested in looking at cyclic patterns that affect people's lives, such as getting a job where the boss turns out to be a complete horror to work with and my client gets fired a few days later, or just quits.

When these same events tend to happen over and over, we are always concerned as to why.

This particular lady was very sensitive to men, especially men in authority. This related to males at work, in school, and even in the general environment as a whole.

She originally had aspirations of becoming a lawyer, but had always run into obstacles when it came time to go before the male-dominated entrance boards of particular schools, breaking down and literally failing her exams.

Men made her feel small and unworthy, and men in authority kept crippling her efforts to move beyond her fears.

This had very real and tangible negative effects on her life.

So we started to work on her subconscious fears, using our exclusive methods.

Through our various muscle tests, it became apparent that this woman had an amazing amount of energy aroused when it came to the subject of cats. Her subconscious mind was telling us what her conscious thoughts couldn't.

She said she had never owned a cat, and didn't have any idea why that particular subject would have any power over her daily life.

Maybe there was some incident with a dog or a pet fish, or maybe a bird?

The muscle testing kept coming back to felines, kitties, and cats.

There was no mistaking the signs for any other animal.

Was it some traumatic event with an internationally loved Japanese cartoon character? Should we say, Hello, Kitty, and start searching for a long-lost, plastic sippy cup?

The testing kept saying that some major event happened to this woman around the age of five or six, and it most assuredly did not involve a beagle or a chihuahua.

I kept asking if she had any memories involving kittens.

Suddenly, as it often happens in our work, she had her eureka moment.

Her facial expression changed from spontaneous joy to massive fear and apprehension.

A curtain to her past had obviously been opened and she was being flooded with long forgotten memories from her distant childhood.

She remembered being five years old and going with her parents to visit an uncle who lived in the scenic countryside.

The woman's mind was immediately back in the

sights, smells and sounds of her sepia-toned memories.

She was feeling the warmth of the sun on her face, hearing the joyous laughs and giggles of her country cousins, seeing the dirt road of her past, and enjoying the precious memories of long-gone family and friends.

My client was once again feeling the youthful energy of her five-year old self, running and jumping with careless abandonment, curious about the world around her and fearless in her pursuit of adventure with her gang of childhood co-conspirators.

While the children explored the world around them, her dad and her uncle were out in the backyard working on a stubborn lawn mower that refused to start, despite their repeated best efforts to produce combustion.

These two worlds were existing side-by-side, with bountiful energy bubbling over among the children, as tensions and frustrations grew among the male adults, fighting a machine that wouldn't ignite.

The joyous rays of the sun that provided warmth and fuel for the children's fantasies, only made the male backyard mechanics hot, thirsty, and increasingly frustrated.

While playing their usual childhood games of chase and hide-n-seek, the kids heard a sound that took their minds entirely off of the games at hand.

Hidden partially out of sight, the children discovered a litter of very young kittens, meowing and purring, the very definition of cute and cuddly.

If anything was ever designed to go together, it has to be a pack of 5-year old cousins and half a dozen newly born bundles of fur with whiskers and little pink nibbling tongues.

The mother cat was nowhere to be seen.

The children started petting and playing with their newfound living, breathing bundles of joy, squealing with laughter at each pink tongue lick and furry tail wag.

Meanwhile, Dad and Uncle Bob continued their fruitless struggles with the lifeless steel excuse for a lawn mower.

Uncle scraped his knuckles on a frozen bolt, and literally shed blood on his work.

Dad offered his expertise and muscle-power to the task at hand, but the motor refused to start.

The client, the then-five year old daughter, picked up one of the cutest of the litter and ran back to show it to her dear father, so extremely proud of her new discovery in the bushes.

She was so happy, she was positively bubbling over with glee. This was so much better than previous times when she had found crawdaddies in the creek, or caught a lightning bug in a fruit jar.

This little kitten had a face and a smile and a tail that never stopped wiggling.

The little girl was besotted with love and affection for her new bestest friend in the entire world.

As she ran towards her loving father, she mentally tried out names in her head for her new fur ball.

Maybe she would call it "Mr. Meow," or "Boots" and "Special Kitty."

Surely her father would let her take "Special Kitty" home with her if she promised to be extra good, do all of her chores, and never, ever ask for anything else the rest of her entire life?

She would water it, and feed it, and make sure it was loved and hugged every hour on the hour of every single day until she became a big girl, got married and left her bedroom to marry her prince on his big white horse.

By then, her little kitty would have furry kittens of her own, and everybody could live together happily ever after just like Snow White, and Cinderella.

All of these joyous thoughts and more flashed through her bobbing head as she dashed towards her father to share the good news.

Uncle Bob was all hot and sweaty, banging away on the useless grass cutter.

Dad's suggestions, while well-meaning, were not producing any results.

My client finally reached her father, proudly cradling the new kittens in her little hands.

She couldn't get the words out of her 5-year old mouth fast enough, rushing and stumbling to share her joy with her father and uncle.

Had she been a little older, she might have noticed the tension and frustrations engulfing the men.

She might have heeded her dad's request to leave them alone, and just go back to playing with her cousins.

Had she been looking at the situation with more mature eyes and less youthful enthusiasm, she might have seen the critical moment when her uncle's aggravation reached the point of no return and became outright rage with deadly consequences.

Her uncle was at his boiling point, and ready to explode.

But my client was too busy loving her new kitty with all of her heart and soul, flooding it with affection and little girl kisses.

She was so enthralled with showing off her new best

friend to her father and uncle, she didn't even have time to react when her uncle's savage hammer blows, previously directed at the dented metal of the ancient lawn mower, were suddenly focused on her precious kitten.

Whereas mere moments before her uncle had been yelling for her to leave them alone, and let them get the lawn mower running, now the little girl was looking at her broken kitten, dying in a pool of crimson blood on the grass, its fragile skull smashed in like a rotten tomato.

Uncle Bob smashed the kitty to pieces with his hammer, taking out his frustrations and solving absolutely nothing.

The kitty was murdered right before my client's young eyes, and the killer had been her very own uncle, who committed his violence under the protective eyes of my client's father.

The horror of that moment came crashing down on the heart of my then five-year old client, and then transcended the decades since to attack my now adult client in the pit of her soul in my office.

It had been over forty years since the innocent kitty was taken from my also innocent client, and the memory had been consciously lost to her as she grew into a woman.

But her subconscious mind never forgot the moment.

Or forgave it.

Is it any wonder that she grew up mistrusting men? Is it a surprise that she had issues with authority figures?

How had the subconscious memories of this horrific event kept her from living the life she always wanted but could never quite achieve?

Can you see why she grew up afraid to ask questions?

Can you see why she had problems showing her emotions to others?

Can you see why she was never really able to trust men and their actions?

We worked on her issues and released this experience with our Shifting Lives Method.

I'm happy to report that today this woman is no longer a secretary, afraid of men in authority, meekly working at a law firm.

Today, she is living her dream of being a lawyer, helping countless people with their own cases and needs.

She was able to get rid of her negative energy, and live the life she deserved.

She freed herself from her doubts and fears, clearing the path for her current and future successes.

Hello, kitty. Goodbye, fears.

That is why we say that here at Shifting Lives, we have a permanent release for your negative beliefs.

Hear, See and Speak No Evil

Due to the nature of our work, we often encounter clients who have already been through the wringer of modern medical efforts usually with less than satisfactory results.

By the time they make it to our door, they have spent hundreds of thousands of dollars on various tests, procedures, medicines, and treatments that simply didn't work.

The clients often view our work as their last best hope to find success, begging for relief from the pain they are enduring.

One prime example occurred about ten years ago when a young woman came to town, and through some friends, walked in our door, initially seeking relief with the use of acupuncture procedures.

When I actually heard the details of her case, I realized her situation involved more than just the symptoms that could be treated by clinical acupuncture work.

She was in her late twenties and had, according to friends and family, just "suddenly" developed a condition where she was losing her hearing by more than fifty percent. And as if this wasn't bad enough, her vision was also diminishing by an equal percentage. And to top it off, her voice was cracking and going away, each day finding it harder and harder for her to speak and convey her thoughts to those around her, with her words becoming almost inaudible.

She was literally going blind, deaf and mute right in front of her family, and there didn't seem to be any logical reason for her worsening condition.

She had been tested, analyzed, probed and prodded by doctors in several states, running up huge medical bills that sapped her energy.

Meanwhile, her condition continued to go steadily downhill, despite the best efforts of some of the top minds and facilities in the nation.

She was losing her ability to connect with the world, and was understandably at her wit's end, each day bringing a new set of horrors and fears to her already fragile system.

By the time she appeared before me, she was ready to jump out of her skin, desperate to leave the increasingly isolated world her damaged body was encasing around her mind.
It was obvious that despite my skill with needles and pressure points, this dear soul needed more than a few

pricks and another bill for services rendered.

I realized that something much deeper was going on with this client.

Knowing how the subconscious mind can affect the physical body, and manifest various conditions, I started asking her about the details of the timeline of her ailments.

I was concerned with how "sudden" her condition developed. Was it literally overnight or did it take weeks to see changes?

It turned out that the situation had been physically developing in her body for over four months, not quite as "suddenly" as I had been lead to believe.

And all this time, she had been seeking medical help from the nation's best in California, Colorado, the East Coast, and beyond.

She was looking for help and basic answers to the crisis, spending all of her resources and more in an attempt to find relief and the reason why these things were happening to her.

She was desperate.

I went back on her timeline, trying to nail down the first moment she noticed these problems developing. She was able to give me a date, a specific moment when she started losing her abilities.

I asked her to tell me the details of what was going on in her life at that moment, and could those events have anything to do with her current handicaps.

I wasn't looking for her to tell me about eating some odd-tasting shellfish, or swimming among glowing orbs of jelly in a pool. I wasn't seeking a "Twilight Zone" moment of green aliens hiding in her closet, or her stepping on an ancient bronze spear, piercing her flesh.

There had to be some specific event that set these symptoms in motion, and I was confident that the answers were in her mind, subconscious or not, just waiting to be revealed.

After some reluctance on her part, in her ever-fading voice, she told me that during this time her parents divorced after a forty year marriage.

The divorce had been very traumatic for the entire family, with decades of resentment and emotions bubbling over.

It was during this time that my client went to visit her father, and he had taken this opportunity to spring a surprise on his daughter, the woman who was now steadily losing her senses, one by one.

The father's new, much younger girlfriend was there, a woman barely the age of my client, and she was openly flaunting her new relationship with my client's father.

Naturally enough, my client felt ambushed, enraged, and betrayed by this confrontation.

She told her father that she didn't want to see him with this person, hear about the new relationship, or talk to him about the new woman in his life ever again.

There was a moment of silence in the room as she recounted the experience.

It was truly a light-bulb-going-off-in-her-head moment. As soon as the words were out of her fragile throat, she realized the answer to her problems was in her own thoughts.

She had manifested her own destiny. Her words of anger to her father became her own reality. A self-created prison, locking her physical senses in a self-imposed jail cell.

Hysterical blindness, deafness, and loss of speech are very real medical conditions, acknowledged by institutes and hospitals around the world.

This isn't the stuff of afternoon talk shows and sensationalism reporting.

Using our Subconscious Release Healing Method, we were able to release her thoughts, and this young woman got her life, and her senses back.

It only took a very few sessions to produce results that had evaded traditional medical practitioners all over the country.

Whereas previous tests, procedures, MRIs, exams had only produced large expenditures, our work gave this woman back her life.

Her symptoms melted away, and the veil of isolation was lifted from her.

She is now happy and healthy, leading a vigorous lifestyle, while traveling around the globe, experiencing the wonders of the world with all five of her fully recovered senses.

All of this came because of her release of subconscious fears that had been robbing her of the life she deserved.

She let go of a very traumatic experience that had hit her like a freight train, and one that had been ignored by modern medicine beliefs that seem to push the latest drug and pharmaceutical miracle as cures.

By dealing with her subconscious mind, we were able to deal with her inner state of being, using the amazing power of her own mind to cure her ailments, and change her outward appearance and experience.

This is the power of our Shifting Lives Method.

The first client in this chapter had a nearly undetectable issue with men in authority that had developed slowly over time, and this issue could have gone unidentified for the remainder of her life.

The woman in the second story had obvious clinically verifiable physical symptoms that manifested quickly and were very obvious to her and to everyone who was around her.

Both of these stories have similar contributing factors, albeit with quite different manifestation of symptoms, and the damaging results are very real in both women's lives.

Let us now look at the less obvious.

We know by the stories that "men in authority" is the underlying factor creating physical and mental distress.

The second issue found in both clients is that of personal power, more correctly, the loss of personal power. Events like those described can and do have a profound effect on one's personal power through a lack of control over events.

Self-esteem and self-worth are both impacted in scenarios like these described due to the destructive nature of emotions attached to authority figures.

Both women gave power to men who were trusted to

lead, guide, and protect them through the frightening moments in their young lives. Even though these men inadvertently and unwittingly betrayed this trust, they were also there for their most fond and happiest moments.

By giving away their personal power, the emotional impact experienced in these highly charged events was extremely devastating.

The energy created by a highly emotional event leaves "wounds" in the psyche *and* in the physical cellular memory, and these "wounds" are forever recorded in the subconscious mind.

The recorded information affects lives in several ways: Immediate physical symptoms like sinus congestion and headaches, delayed emotional inconsistencies, unbalanced behavior, and sometimes seemingly unrelated behaviors like rage, addictions, and depression.

The threads of memories attached to people, places, and events can be hidden deep within the psyche and affect areas of life that would otherwise have no connection to past experiences.

The subconscious can and does link past memories to current events. Like the finest computer, it can scan records in a millisecond and offer an opinion or judgment related to the current circumstance.

Thousands of people are living lives that are being

directed and controlled by hidden unseen forces that are in turn influenced by the experiences, events, and beliefs recorded in the subconscious mind.

The body is an outward expression of your inner state of being.

~ Dr. Keith South ~

Chapter Two

Fear of Men

Taking a Right Turn

We don't treat addictions. We treat people.

While that might seem like a simple explanation for a complex problem, it is proven to be true every day in our work with our Subconscious Release Healing Method.

We were working with a client of ours, dealing with substance abuse, and in the course of our muscle testing, it came to light that a major event had happened to her in her childhood that was still affecting her today.

We had targeted her age at this time period, and were working on determining the person doing the action. Was it her mother, father, sister or maybe a friend?
In this particular case, our client remembered her

grandfather coming to pick her up for their regular outing together

Granddad put her in his trusty ole pickup truck and drove off down the familiar road to the family homestead.

Every other time, her Granddad would take the left turn in the road at this one section, and they would soon be enjoying a big glass of lemonade and maybe a piece of Grandmother's famous peach cobbler.

But not this time.

For some reason unknown to my client, who was then a young girl, Grandfather took a turn to the right, going down a different path.

They came up to a little cabin that the young girl had never seen before.

Where was Grandma and her big smile? Did she forget to make a pie this week? Had they moved out of the big old farmhouse with all of those wonderful smells and great hiding places?

This little cabin was much too small to hold all of the furniture that filled every room to overflowing in the other house.

My client kept asking her trusted guardian why they were going to this new place, but then the memory would get fuzzy, and we would lose the moment.

During the initial round of testing, it seemed that she had a memory of flashing lights and a vague feeling of uneasiness. She felt like she was back in some bedroom, and she didn't know why she was there. Her visions weren't distinct or focused enough to resolve the questions.

We kept hitting roadblocks in our efforts, not sure if we were going down the right path to our mental destination.

We kept testing her subconscious mind with our methods, and suddenly had a breakthrough of specific memories.

It turned out that Grandfather was seeing another woman for some afternoon delights, while Grandma was busy making pies back in her own kitchen.

He had taken his girlfriend down to the creek bank for some adult activities, leaving my client, who at the time was only a five year old girl, by herself, unprotected in the now empty cabin. Mother and father were unaware of their daughter's peril and did not know of the rapist in the area.

A rambling hobo-type homeless man had seen the little girl alone through the window, and seized the opportunity to walk in and rape my client while she was totally defenseless.

The memories she had of flashing lights were those of the policemen who had been called when her limp and damaged body had been discovered by her returning Grandpa and his girlfriend.

Fortunately the rapist had been caught, and his series of crimes had been put to a stop, but not in time to save my client and her innocence.

This entire episode had been suppressed for decades by my client, but the damage never went away.

Her body healed, but her mind and emotions did not.

All she remembered of the event was Granddad turning the wrong way on the normal trip home to his house.

We released this negative energy from her subconscious mind, freeing the negative charge she held on this event.

Immediately her substance abuse stopped, and her damaged relationship with her estranged husband started to be repaired and healed.

Her trust issues resolved themselves, and her entire outlook on life was renewed with a clarity she hadn't experienced in decades.

Her trust in men increased, and her relationships came back together.

Clearing even memories that aren't consciously remembered can have a profound effect on people's lives.

This is a fundamental part of our Shifting Lives Method, and it is available to all of our clients in need.

---Review---

The main theme of this story may seem obvious: fear of men, fear of abusive men, and addictive behavior.

This experience goes much deeper than the surface level. The emotions involved in this case are control, fear, paralyzed will, anger, abandonment, low self-esteem, and instability.

Our client felt helpless due to "lack of control over events", but it really goes much deeper than that.

Due to the nature of our work, we often have to use words that define subconscious scenarios from the subconscious point of view.

In this example, the word *control* is the contrast that the subconscious created in an attempt to explain how she was treated by the rapist. The parents did nothing out of the ordinary, but we are talking about the child's perception from the subconscious mind point of view.

She was controlled by the inability to make a choice as to where her grandfather took her, and she was also physically unable to overcome the power of the rapist.

The emotion of fear again may seem apparent, but let's look deeper as it pertains to this event. The fear experienced by our young client was spread out among several different aspects of her life.

It affected her relationships, physical body, sexual relationships, personal power, and personality.

Fear, as we all know, can be a crippling emotion. Yet, do we consider that fear can have an effect on our daily activities of life some twenty-five years later?

It shows up in marital breakdown, drug abuse, difficulties at work, and interpersonal relationships with all people.

In this women's life, fear was a destructive force paralyzing her every effort to live a normal life.

"Paralyzed Will" may not be a familiar term. Will comes from a creative place in the mind, and some say it comes from our deep innate reasoning faculties.

Feelings of fear, doubt, worry, and over concern for the opinion of others can and does limit our creative power which expresses itself as will.
Therefore in this story the lasting effects of "Paralyzed Will" severely stifled our client's ability to express heartfelt emotions, to trust others, and to love others including herself.

Anger is another emotion present in this case.

This may seem obvious to most of us reading this story, and I believe that the effect of anger in this example runs deep within the psyche.

Her anger was so profound that nearly all memory of this event was stuffed deep into a place of no return and walled off behind some curtain of protection created to lessen the pain accumulated by the horrific tragedy she experienced.

Her anger spewed out onto everyone in her life and was so apparent it may as well have been written on her face like the Scarlet Letter.

The feeling of "Abandoned" showed up in her everyday life. It showed up as a lack of trust, and it also showed up as a feeling of isolation like being left out of parties and social gatherings.

The weird thing is subconsciously she really didn't want to attend them anyway, but she felt lonely, hurt, and insulted when not asked to attend a party.

Jung said it best when he stated, "That which you resist persists."

With abandonment issues, the emotion persists with a vengeance due to the lack of desire to become intimate with others. This all comes from a deep place of fear including the fear of the person leaving.

Our client had low self-esteem, even though, she had no full conscious memory of the long ago occurrence causing her issues.

She did however have this feeling of being different. She described somehow feeling dirty, not worthy to be close to others, distant, and needing to run away from activities at school.

She did find refuge with the drug crowd, and she was fully accepted among the let's-get-high-and-party group.

So this became her life wrecking any hope for a career, relationship, real friends, and a normal family life.

The emotion of "Instability" expressed itself in nearly all aspects of her life, as well as, affecting relationships, work, finances, and her health.

Keep on going and chances are you will
stumble on something, perhaps when you are
least expecting it. I never heard of anyone
ever stumbling on something sitting down.

~ Charles F Kettering ~

Chapter Three

Discovering the Artist & Hidden Creativity

Singing A New Tune

One of the joys of my working with our Shifting Lives Method is the opportunity it gives me to help creative people in their careers.

Over the years, I've been fortunate to offer aid and assistance to various musicians, writers, artists, and numerous others who pursue creative outlets for their talents.

I've helped people at every level of their careers, dealing with clients at the very top of their fields with international levels of success on down to starving, homeless artists who didn't have two nickels to rub together.

The creative fields are often feast or famine.
Cities like Los Angeles, New York and Nashville are

filled with tens of thousands of vibrant souls riding the endless roller coasters of fame and then forgotten, stars making millions of dollars one year, then pawning their treasures and running from the bill collectors the next.

In a time when even proven talented entertainers are losing their deals and contracts, it is seldom a case of not being good enough. Buses roll into towns every day filled with people who are good enough.

The world is filled with talented people, but talent alone often isn't enough

A few years ago, I had the experience of working with a musician friend of mine that I have known for over fifteen years.

This extremely talented man showed up at my doorstep one day with his life literally in his hands. His guitar case, holding the tool of his profession, was in one hand, and everything else he owned in this world was in a worn canvas sack thrown over his shoulder.

He was homeless and penniless, operating in a dazed and confused mode that was barely functional.

He was the very definition of down and out, running on empty.

Like so many other hopefuls, he had come to Nashville, Tennessee, Music City USA, to conquer the record industry and become a household name.

He had beaten the odds of the countless other wannabes by actually getting signed to a deal with a major record label.

He had done some studio work, recorded a few of his songs, and was starting to live his dream of making a living in the music industry.

Then just as fast, his project was shelved, and he was out of work. Soon after, he was out of money, and running on vapors, scrambling to just keep himself alive

So we took the opportunity to do our exclusive Shifting Lives Method, and over the course of about six weeks, working very diligently on his self-esteem, we removed all of his fears, judgments and doubts.

One day we had this amazing breakthrough event.

It was a sad situation involving his father and some issues of abuse in a rural environment, involving alcohol and physical violence.

He had this explosive release, physically let go of all of his pain and anguish surrounding this event.

Less than two weeks after this release, he was signed to new major record label.

The label put a huge amount of money and resources behind him, sending him out on a national radio tour to introduce his music to listeners.

Within a couple of months his album went Top Ten, his video went Top Ten, and his life totally turned around in the best ways possible.

Today he is an award-winning performer with more money than he can imagine, the admiration of his peers and the dedicated support of his legions of fans.

Even the most casual of music fans know his name, and he has become a fixture on talk shows, awards presentations, and the red carpets of the entertainment world.

Since our initial work with him, we've also been able to help members of his band, his road crew, and his family, sharing the positive results of our Shifting Lives Method.

And you have no idea how much we would love to share his name with you. We wish we could show you our framed plaque of his gold records, and the treasured photo of the three of us smiling and showing our love for one another. For some reason his management team thinks we should keep the secret to his success quiet for the time being.

Just know that the same methods that turned this artist's life around are now available to you and yours.

Up, Up and Away

A lady in her mid-sixties came to our office last year suffering from almost crippling back pain.

Though it wasn't apparent at first, the source of her pain was an incident that happened to her in the scenic cornfields of Kansas, thirty-five years prior to her visit with us.

It didn't involve a scarecrow or a dog named Toto, but it revolved around a hot air balloon and her fear of abandonment.

She had gone on a trip with a group of friends to experience the exciting sensations of taking a ride in a colorful hot air balloon, planning to enjoy floating on the breeze across the windswept prairies of middle America.

As her companions climbed into the ornate wicker basket, she cast her eye on the billowing silk envelope over her head, filling with heated air and rising up to meet the sun.

Soon she would be floating among the clouds, racing the local birds on the winds of the land, casting her fate to whatever direction the gods provided.

Her excitement kept building, as her friends claimed various positions in the now rising basket, still tethered to the ground by thick ropes of nylon.

Maybe it was due to a sudden burst of wind, or maybe one of her friends simply moved to the side too rapidly, but for whatever reason, just as she was attempting to steady herself on the edge of the basket, the entire five-story tall balloon of heated air shook, sending a tremor through the vehicle.

Our client lost her footing and tumbled out of the wicker gondola, falling flat out on the Kansas prairie ground.

The sudden loss of her 135 pounds of ballast caused the balloon to leap up into the sky, breaking the restraints of the tether lines, sending the party of friends and the pilot up, up and away.

Except for our client.

As the hot air balloon bolted towards the heavens, our client watched in horror from below, her body in a ditch she created with her untimely fall, while bits of hay and dirt partially softened her descent.

Her friends were soon little more than tiny colorful dots, swishing away from sight, while she lay crippled in the corn rows.

Whereas seconds earlier she had been surrounded by friends and a skilled hot air balloon pilot, she now found herself recoiling in pain, alone and abandoned, as even the ground crew had left in hot pursuit of the newly airborne vehicle.

She was alone and without even a wizard to ooze her back to health. Where was Auntie Em when she really needed her?

When would her friends realize she wasn't with them?

Would anybody ever be able to find her in that field of corn?

How could she survive such obstacles when she wasn't even sure if she could get up and walk, feeling only the piercing pain shooting up and down the length of her legs?

While she obviously was rescued eventually, her ordeal was far from over.

She spent the next several decades having tests and x-rays, dealing with chronic back pain issues.

Her doctors kept trying to find physical reasons for her intense suffering.

They kept coming up short, failing to bring my client any relief.

They failed to realize that the reasons for her pain were hidden behind subconscious curtains.

They were busy looking for obvious reasons, and ignoring the wizard behind the scenes pinching her nerves.

The human body is the outward expression of our inner state of being.

We did one of our Shifting Lives Method sessions on this lady, and the subject of the hot air balloon incident in that Kansas cornfield so many years ago, never came up.

We did find numerous experiences involving low self esteem and confidence issues, leading us to test for abandonment feelings in her past.

This line of testing revealed her agony of being crippled in the cornfield as her friends soared away before her eyes, off on exciting adventures of discovery and fulfillment, while she lay bruised and broken in the dirt.

She was able to remember exactly how she felt, waiting those agonizing 45-minutes while the ground crew anxiously searched for her injured body, once the balloon's pilot realized she had prematurely exited the wicker basket.

She had subsequently spent years taking medicines and ointments, seeking relief from her non-stop agony, enduring countless painful sessions of physical therapy and treatments.

But her pain never went away.

We looked at her anxiety and feelings of abandonment, taking note of her low self-esteem, and literally during the course of one session, her back pain went away.

The hour we spent focusing on the cause of her pain proved more effective than decades of effort devoted to treating her symptoms.

She called us the next day saying that she had been able to get out of her bed that morning for the first time in 35 years, without having to endure crippling pain that robbed her of her personal power and zest for life.

To this day, now over a year since our first session, her back pain has never come back.

While we make no universal claim that this solution is the cure-all for every person's back pain, we know first-hand that our client's subconscious had held her captive for over 35 years, paralyzing her life with fears and negative energy. Her emotional state had been held iron-clad for almost four decades before we were able to release it from her subconscious mind and shift her life with lasting results.

We can proudly say she wasn't stuck in the cornfields of Kansas anymore.

Bad Back for Business

As so often happens in my clinic, I had a client come in with one set of problems that turned out to just be the tip of the iceberg as to the real issue.

This man had a bad back. On the surface that sounds pretty common. It wasn't any exotic ailment that only shows up in the scripts of some far-fetched television hospital drama, requiring a team of the world's most inquisitive minds, racing the clock to determine some obscure disease just in time for the fourth commercial break.

No, this gentleman had an aching back, and he needed some relief to his constant pain.
While working on his muscles and bones, I had the opportunity to interview him about some patterns that seemed to be defining his life, and perhaps causing some of his aches.

Using my Shifting Lives Method, I quickly determined that this man seemed to be attracting certain negative elements into his life repeatedly.

This man was a real entrepreneur; in fact, I think he could safely be called a serial entrepreneur, always starting new business ventures, one right after another.

He had seemingly done it all; opening restaurants, operating a car lot, running a landscaping business, and even developing a movie rental outlet.

All of his enterprises had failed.

You might be tempted to say that this fine fellow had simply had a bad run of luck.

All of these projects would start out with great promise, showing all of the initial signs of becoming lasting success stories, building up momentum.

Then a series of unusual things would happen, snatching defeat from the jaws of victory.

He would have issues with licenses, problems with suppliers, zoning difficulties, leases that turned out to be horrible, all sorts of things that while common business headaches, would turn into fatal mistakes for his fledgling enterprises.

The fact that these things kept happening to my client regardless of the kinds of businesses he created. These little incidents could possibly happen once or twice to somebody. But he turned them into a full-blown trend that wore him down physically and emotionally. He assumed it was the other person's issues, when in fact, they were his own.

The only common denominator in these unrelated projects was the man himself.

I did some muscle testing to see what was hidden in the recesses of my client's subconscious mind, and soon discovered he had major issues with his own self-esteem and self-worth.

Digging a little deeper into his background, I discovered that he wasn't raised in the best of backgrounds.

He had a father that was abusive, and was never one to encourage my client, then a boy. Failing to acknowledge his successes to make my client feel better about his efforts, resulted in him becoming defensive in his relationships. His personal power had been harmed by the extreme control exhibited by his father, and as a result he had a "paralyzed will".

My client was carrying around a large set of baggage dealing with his questions about being worthy of success.

He had the energy.

He had the motivation to go and create these various enterprises.

He just didn't have the staying power needed to keep his companies successful, viable, and liquid enough to move them forward.

After several sessions doing the work I do, revealing the various aspects of his life that were causing the self-esteem issues, plus some concerns about abandonment, more on an emotional level than actual physical absence, I found out that my client's father simply didn't know how to show affection and support.

This wasn't a cut on his father's personality or communication on a most basic level, one that had entered my client's childhood subconscious mind and never left.

The purpose of my exploration was not to point fingers at my client's family and cry boo-hoo tears about what a horrible life he had.

It was to identify the problems paralyzing my client in his adult life, and release them from their place of control.

These long forgotten issues were coloring my client's daily decisions and affecting not only his world and security, but those of his friends and family.

Our Shifting Lives Method neutralized his negative energy, taking a bad experience that was weighing down on my client, causing emotional and physical problems that were real and tangible, clearing it out and releasing all of his instabilities.

It didn't change the history of his life. It just changed his reactions and gave him a different outlook by erasing those limiting beliefs, opening him up to reveal the possibilities that were inside his amazingly entrepreneurial mind.

His case is not unique.

I believe that inside every one of us there is a successful, creative, energetic spirit, capable of producing amazing Earth-changing works if we can just peel away the many negative layers of experiences we have had with others on planet earth.

Every one of us is a unique spirit, waiting to be set free.

Here at Shifting Lives, we have a permanent release for your negative beliefs.

---Review---

In each of these stories, there is a common thread to be found, a thread that runs deep within the psyche.

"Self worth" and "Self-Esteem" are often spoken of as one and the same.

In our work, there is need for differentiation between the two.

"Self-Esteem" is the outward image portrayed to the world, whereas, self worth is that critical view of self that one sees in the mirror late at night while alone.

"Personal power" is that all-important part of our psychological makeup that allows the creative forces to flow through us. This power is sometimes given away to another person because of our own guilt or self-punishment, and sometimes, it is given away for self-preservation.

Releasing the artist within is a symbolic term associated with the core creative force within each of us. Sometimes this force is deeply suppressed due to childhood trauma, fear, feeling unloved, or "Timid/Miffed." Parents, teachers, and society are the usual suppressors that squelch the artist within.

The following are the emotions affecting the individuals in these examples: control, "Timid/Miffed," unloved, and low self worth.

For the musician and our business man, a controlling parent was the initial catalyst that sent their lives into a tailspin. Though our balloonist lady had a major life event set off the destructive force of control, the end result was much the same in the form of a life shaped by beliefs influencing the conscious mind.

"Timid/Miffed" is revealed as suppressing their ability to perform limiting the creative aspects of their lives.

"Timid," as a general description and as it pertains to our work, is suppressed anger, unspoken feelings, and fear to express one's true feeling.

In each of these cases, our story participants were unable, unwilling, or incapable of releasing the pent up emotions trapped inside.

Remember, it does not matter if our example case studies were indeed loved or unloved. It is merely a conclusion created in their own mind based on appearances and evidence compiled by the subconscious mind. The feeling of being unloved is very real to the one that is feeling it, and it often gets transferred to many aspects of their lives.

Self worth is a major contributing factor in each of these scenarios. The self worth issues of our singer and businessman were crushed by unloving mentally abusive fathers.

Year after year of never being good enough to satisfy the impossible demands of an angry, hostile, and even violent guardian took its toll.

Whereas, the offender in the case of our balloon lady was her life threatening fall. The self-imposed damage is still quite real and equally destructive. Deep grooves are etched into the fragile minds of the person expressing low self worth.

The aspects of life affected in each of these stories are much the same.

Money was certainly a major concern in each case, seriously restricted in the musician's and the businessman's lives.

Allowing himself to have a home was a theme in the singer's life.

Our balloonist had physical pain every day of her life for thirty-five years.

Resentment and lack of forgiveness was prevalent in all three of our examples.

Greed was a huge contributing factor in the life experience of the businessman, as if somehow money could ease the pain of his undesirable childhood.

*Tell him to live by yes and no; yes to
everything good, and no to everything bad.*

~ William James ~

Chapter Four

Inner Conflict

A Tale of Two Athletes

This is a story of two talented football players who had almost equal talents but ended up with lives of extreme opposites.

In my career I've had the opportunity to work with numerous world-class athletes over the years, champions in their fields who were truly amazing people.

I've discovered that successful sportsmen are usually very driven and goal-oriented. They have focus and determination, which compliments their athletic talents, leading to a massive will to overcome obstacles.

Just imagine two young men coming out of college at the same time. They are both great football players with proven success on the field.

They both just happen to be running backs.

Both players are immediately drafted by professional teams, turning each of them into instant millionaires.

These men are similar in age, similar in build, and are both expected to bring their NFL teams great success in upcoming seasons.

One of our players goes on to have twelve solid years of amazing success, both on the field and off.

He makes smart business decisions, spectacular plays on the turf, and earns tens of millions for his family and future security.

Life is good, and he enjoys his moments in the spotlight, counting his blessings as his golden touch continues in his post-game life with business associates who value his efforts off the field almost as much as his time wearing a jersey.

He has the dream life that everybody imagines a pro athlete should have.

Then we have the story of the other player.

His life didn't turn out anything like he had hoped for when he dreamed his dreams on the college turf.

The very first day of practice in his new role as a professional NFL layer, he blew his knee out and lost his entire career. His knee was shot and could not be repaired. His life as he knew it was over before it even really started.

So what was the difference between these two men?

You can say that the second player simply had a weak knee and couldn't handle requirements of his chosen profession.

He had a bad break, was just unlucky, and came up short on the deck of life.

That is certainly one way to look at things.

I contend there is another possibility to be examined.

In our minds we have these tapes running that carry our past experiences, modeling our behavior.

All of the things we say and experience, especially the events in our early years, creep into our subconscious minds and govern our following actions.

In the example of my successful player who received the rewards, had the mansion, earned million for his efforts, all of his success was congruent with the thoughts in his subconscious mind.

The other player with his so-called "bad luck" was like so many athletes who veered off their paths and self-destructed.

We all have these negative thoughts in our subconscious minds that are affecting our daily actions, our self-worth and our personal power.

In our work with the athlete who blew out his knee and lost his career, we discovered that he was abused as a child, lived in poverty, and was even misused by family members when his budding talent was discovered on the football field.

He faced pressures he was never prepared to absorb, taking on the role of saving his entire family's fortune with his athletic skills.

Even though his physical body allowed him to become a successful person on the playing fields of high school and college, there was a limiting belief that he was never going to be successful adult with five million dollars in the bank.

His subconscious mind said no to that possibility, convincing his body that it was just not going to happen, and that is why his knee failed him at precisely the right/wrong time.

The physical body is an outward expression of our inner state of being.

These facts apply to all athletes, not just football players. The same issues apply to tennis players, soccer players, basketball players, and others.

Golf is especially a game of the mind.

If a golfer can get right up there at the top of the leader board, with the right mind set he can win the tournament.

How many times have we seen players fall apart at the last possible moment due to some unknown lack of focus? On a weekly basis, we see top-flight golfers self-destruct with cyclic patterns that the subconscious mind reproduces, trying to heal them of negative energy and limiting thoughts.

Our conscious minds are trying to reveal the negative tapes stored in the unconscious and clean out our negative memories allowing subconscious release healing.

In our work, we are shifting lives by offering a permanent release to your negative beliefs.

Bad Road Trip Memories

Life is filled with endless decisions, offering various paths and choices.

One of my clients discovered that he had literally been taking the wrong turn for over 30 years due to a tragic event in his teens.

He entered my office about twelve years ago, unknowingly suffering from an experience he had endured when he was involved in a car wreck with his girlfriend at the time, some 24 years earlier.

He came to my office seeking relief for various neck and back pains, believing them to be delayed results from his road accident.

It turned out that those pains were only part of the lingering problems he retained from the car crash.

The story began when he was sixteen, driving his parents' car, showing off for his young girlfriend in the passenger seat, cruising down a scenic back road a little too fast for even an experienced driver, much less a teenage rookie.

While talking with his gal, he missed a curve, sending the car flying off the hillside, wrapping it around a tree.

They found themselves hurt and trapped inside his family's station wagon, out of sight from the road in these days before cell phones and GPS tracking systems.

Both of them could and should have probably died out there in the middle of nowhere, waiting for help.

Somehow he managed to peel himself out of the wreckage and make his way back up the hillside to wait for help from a passing Good Samaritan.

His young girlfriend was more seriously injured than he was, and spent months in the hospital, facing several touch-and-go moments where her very survival was in question.

Even when the situation improved to the point where her survival seemed likely, there were fears that her brain might have been too severely damaged for her to ever regain consciousness or live any semblance of her former existence.

Not surprisingly, this ordeal created a monstrous rift between the two families, resulting in lawsuits and enough litigation to keep teams of lawyers burning the midnight oil.

He came to me as a 40 year old man with neck pain and a bad back, and decades of excess baggage.

The memory of the car wreck was certainly in his mind. He hadn't been able to bury it within the hidden corners of his subconscious, and go about his life.

He was constantly aware of the pain and suffering his earlier lack of judgment and driving skills had caused far too many people.

So he understood why he limped and had pains.

He knew they were lasting souvenirs of his tragic accident.

This much was all on the surface, readily visible to anybody who cared to look at the man's sad history.

But there was something else about this client's actions that caught my curiosity.

It began when he first called to book his appointment, asking for directions to our office.

Now this wasn't unusual in and of itself. He was a new client, had never been to our facilities, and didn't know our section of town.

But his line of questions went far beyond a normal person's queries when asking directions.

Most people only care about getting to the building in question.

This man wanted to know which way he was supposed to turn when he got out of his car, and started walking to the doorway. This detailed question had been preceded by a turn-by-turn set of instructions to even get him into the parking lot in the first place.

They weren't the kind of questions you'd normally hear from an adult driver, more like the innocent and endless bantering from an energetic kindergarten student.

It was just odd.

We decided to probe a little deeper into this specific issue, and soon discovered that this man was suffering from a severe case of dyslexia, far beyond any case I'd previously encountered.

The thought crossed my mind that perhaps this was the reason for his tragic teenage driving mistake on the hillside road so many years ago.

To my surprise he said he didn't recall having any previous issues with writing or typing prior to his accident.

In fact, he didn't even think his symptoms developed until after the wreck, during the turmoil of recovery and the anguish of the court dealings between the two families.

His spatial difficulties concerning which door to enter and which turn to take developed and intensified in the following decades, growing into obvious issues with each passing year.

During our Subconscious Release Healing Method, we focused on this issue and released his guilt, anxiety, fears, and doubts related to the accident and his girlfriend's painful recovery.

We found a permanent release for his negative beliefs, and were finally able to bring some literal direction to his life.

Both of these stories contain examples of "evidence - versus - appearance" [explained in detail in chapter 7] where we see life through our own unique filters. This is the only way to understand how two similar people with such similar backgrounds can have such varied outcomes in their lives.

The emotions involved in these stories are "fear, timid/miffed, abandoned and instability." The fears are presented through the expression of doubt and worrying over the outcome of the unknown.

In each case the unknown is the specific outcome of the discussions made by other people. For the football players, it is which teams that they will ultimately play for? Will they start? Will they become famous? Will they meet the girls of their dreams?

For our auto accident example, will the girl friend live? Will she walk again? Will the family suffer due to the impact of the lawsuit?

Fear can be, and is debilitating in our examples. It revealed itself in seemingly different ways but not really so much differently. Each man reacted differently to the external stimulus. Our one player faced his fears, stepped up, took charge, and pressed through the obstacles to success. Our second player cracked under pressure, and broke at the knee.

Our auto driver created a shield around himself in the form of dyslexia spatial relationship issues to wall off the pain.

We all view the world through our own unique filters.

Timid/miffed is a unique emotion in and of itself. It is most often caused due to unexpressed anger. Being mad enough to scream or fight but keeping the anger inside is a prime example. From the view of modern society it may be best to hold your anger, swallow your word, or bite your tongue, but for some timid/miffed rears its ugly head in other ways: such as spouse abuse, drug abuse, or anti-social behavior. In this case timid/miffed revealed itself through physical dysfunction.

Anger was explained in the timid/miffed section with the possible exception of the deep stirring felt deep within the inner recesses of the second player's mind. He also harbored resentment for the doctors and the team. Unexpressed anger becomes resentment over time.

Abandonment reveals itself through the appearance of failure on the part of our second athlete. He felt abandoned by his team, his family who held extremely high expectations for his success, the life he had fantasized about, expensive cars, and beautiful women.

Our driver felt abandoned by his family and his very senses, not to mention his first love.

Instability reveals as lack of control over events. This involves having to accept the circumstances as they present themselves, despite the once grand enthusiasm that surrounded the dream. Instability can and does affect hundreds of aspects of our lives.

Various aspects of lives affected by the events were described. Some are obvious, like careers, and physical bodies.

Let's look at the less obvious.

In the case of the second football player his spiritual self was greatly affected. He began to doubt God. He wasn't certain if he could allow himself to even consider that there is a God.

What kind of God would allow him to reach such grand heights in high school and college, and then cut the rug from beneath him just as the pay off was about to happen?

"Resentment" is also a huge issue in both of our examples, resentment directed toward self for the mistakes made.

Resentment towards the world because of demands that consume the average man is also a huge issue.

Misplaced anger creating resentment runs deep into the psyche of damaged men.

"Unforgiveness" presents in these examples, showing itself in a somewhat obscure way.

Each of our personal examples had the opportunity to pull themselves up by the boot straps and get on with their lives. Yet the deep pain sustained by their misactions left deep voids at the very core of their beings. Unforgiveness is the poison one drinks hoping the other person dies.

One more topic to discuss is "Greed."

I know that this aspect of live will challenge your knowledge, your thought that you have been following along quite well to this point. You are not sure who was greedy.

Greed shows itself in the example of the second ball player in the following way: he had created expectations of the sport, his team and himself. He had abandoned his love for the game and began instead to boost himself up in prideful ways. Making statements such as "watch me, when I have money I will be somebody. I'll show all of those who pushed me around when I was young, you'll see."

"Pride goeth before a fall."

Forgiveness is the fragrance the violet sheds
on the heel of the one that crushed it.

~ Mark Twain ~

Chapter Five

Love Relationships

Married to the Wrong Person

This might be a familiar type of story for you. Perhaps you know someone this has happened to, or you might actually be the person experiencing this drama over and over.

This concerns a woman who is quite simply married to the wrong man. And not for the first time, or even the second.

This pattern of choosing the wrong person has continued the entire adult life of this woman.
You might be thinking that perhaps she was just unfortunate in love.

I maintain there is a common denominator that causes people to keep making the wrong choices over and over.

I had a lady come to my office and this pattern kept showing up repeatedly in her life.

She would find this wonderful guy, and tell all of her friends that she had finally met Mr. Right, her prince, her knight in shining armor, the one person who could come in and save the day.

Then within a relatively short period time, usually less than ninety days, she would discover various kinks in the armor of Mr. Wonderful. There would be issues that were less than desirable, and her perfect world would come crumbling apart.

Working with this client, using our Shifting Lives Method, we were able to discover what her motivating factors were.

There were real reasons for her bad choices.

She just didn't realize them.

The common denominator in all of her tortured relationships was our client herself.

One of the main issues causing these bad choices was my client's low self-worth, but not necessarily issues with her self-esteem.

These deep-seated hidden core issues went all of the way back into her early childhood.

She had feelings of being unloved, combined with issues concerning abandonment.

On a subconscious level, she just didn't feel worthy of having a relationship with a real Mr. Right, due to her childhood modeling and how her parents treated her. There were even issues with her siblings.

And they weren't huge explosive events that rocked the very foundations of her world. They were little, seemingly insignificant occurrences that happen to millions of children each and every day. But these events affected her childhood, her young adult years, and continued to hinder her adult decisions.

By going into her subconscious, we were able to determine how various events shaped her feelings and perceptions, the very things that caused her to keep making the same bad choices over and over in her adult life.

Even though she couldn't remember the exact information sequences, the thought processes were there, leading her conscious actions.

Think of your subconscious as a computer hard drive where every thought is either a one or a zero, true or false. Your subconscious thoughts are either congruent or incongruent.

When we do our workshops and ask for a volunteer from the audience to demonstrate this concept, we often seek an attractive woman as our example, asking her about her success with relationships.

We ask her what she wants most in life?

Often, her answer will be that she wants a man, so she can be in a successful relationship.

We then ask if she likes men?

She replies that of course she likes men, proclaiming again that is why she wants to be in a love relationship.

Then we ask if she trusts men?

She replies that of course she does. Men are trustworthy. She feels good about that statement.

Then using our exclusive muscle testing, asking the subconscious mind a series of questions with yes or no answers, we quickly discover that the answer is usually no, a resounding no to each of the above questions.

Sometimes even the response to liking men is an undeniable negative on a subconscious level.

Now imagine the reaction from our eager volunteer, recoiling in horror from the results of our muscle test, proclaiming that the tests can't be true, protesting a little bit too loudly that she honestly and genuinely likes men.

When we shift the questions back to those concerning her relationships, asking her to describe her most recent love affair, or even better, her previous two or three entanglements, we start seeing this amazing pattern of bad choices and hopeless situations.

She picks the wrong man, thinking he is her answer to everything wrong in her world, and then after a brief honeymoon of optimism and hopefulness, the pattern repeats and repeats, until Mr. Wonderful's shiny armor is dented, pitted, and smeared with the rotten smell of despair.

Mr. Perfect becomes a horrible person, tossed to the decomposing heap of missed enchantment.

He wasn't anything like she thought he was.

How could she have been so blind, so deceived, so utterly and completely misguided?

It kept coming back to her. She was the face in the mirror, searching for a permanent fix to her rose-colored glasses.

Once we worked on the framework in her subconscious mind, the results were astounding.

Her subconscious mind had been calling out to these negative scenarios, attracting them into her life, bringing in the experiences most needed to reveal the damaged areas of her core beliefs, resting deep within the subconscious mind.

The subconscious mind is an amazing enabler of manifestations, creating things in people's lives, bringing people a mirror showing them what they want to do and what they can do, acting as a reflection of self, so people can heal.

Once these patterns are identified, our Shifting Lives Method offers people a permanent release to their negative beliefs.

Thirty-five Years of Guilt

A woman in her early sixties came into our office one day. She was very attractive and well-dressed.

She had been single for the past 35 years, despite expressing a strong desire to have a loving relationship with a man.

This was puzzling on many levels. She had the appearance, means and motivation to be involved with somebody to a serious degree, and was even socially connected within her community.

While conducting our Shifting Lives Method, exploring and asking questions, we discovered that she had a huge amount of distrust for men.

She unconsciously believed that men were unreliable and simply couldn't be counted on.

As we continued our work, we found issues with sex in a broad term, uncovering guilt and feelings of being violated during the sex act.

We discovered that she had a typical background in that she had dated a little in high school, and then married her true love early in her college years.

This woman had been an artist prior to marriage, and was very gifted in her skills and talents.

Her husband was also an artist, but had less natural skills and creativity.

Our client had placed her own artistic career on hold when she married, and had gone to work in an office to help support her "starving artist," while also finding time to be the loving housewife, keeping the home running.

Over the years, her guilt grew at the sacrifices she had made for the sake of her marriage.

Her passion for art had been put away while her husband struggled to earn a living as a commercial artist doing work for hire.

Our client followed the traditional role of being the supportive wife, allowing this construct to cripple her dreams and aspirations.

She became successful in the business world, applying her natural talents to the details of enterprise.

Meanwhile, her husband's art career never took off.

Locked in our client's subconscious was the belief that the man was the breadwinner, responsible for paying the bills, providing shelter, keeping a roof over their heads.

That was the way she thought things should be, following the examples seen on such television shows as "Father Knows Best," "Ozzie and Harriet," and "Leave It To Beaver."

She broke that tradition by giving up her dreams and going to work in an office to support her marriage.

As often happens in life, they suffered various misfortunes, and their marriage dissolved.

She found herself alone and single.

She had her skills learned from work, and had advanced her fortunes and responsibilities in her job, but her marriage had ended.

She was still young, attractive, and highly eligible, but once the divorce was finalized, she refused to allow herself to get involved with any other man.

Thirty plus years later, she is in our office, still single and alone, with no true explanation for her self-imposed solitude.

She told us that she did in fact meet men in her work and social settings, but the encounters seldom even turned into lunch dates, much less budding romances. She couldn't even remember a time where a second meal had been shared with the same man.

With our Shifting Lives Method we discovered that her past issues of guilt over putting her artistic career on hold were continuing to affect her lack of intimacy with any new prospects for decades.

Probing a little deeper, we soon determined that this successful, vibrant, attractive business executive also didn't have any real friendships with women.

Even her family members were kept at arms' length, never allowed inside this woman's wall of defense.

Her emotions and thought processes were keeping her isolated from the world around her.

We did our work and releases, and almost immediately, our client started attracting worthy men into her life.

She also developed better and more fulfilling friendships with her female associates.

She came more active in her church and the community, sharing her talents, skills and positive energy with the world around her.

She found her creativity, and new outlets for her passion.

One day she dropped by our office saying she had just come from a local art supply house, having bought some blank canvas, paints and brushes.

The artist within her had been reborn, and she couldn't wait to get to work, creating and expressing her long dormant talents and passions.

These are the things that can happen when clients shift their lives, and find permanent release for their negative beliefs.

Pushing Away

Sometimes we encounter a client with patterns that are so obvious that even she knew it, as did her friends.

Unlike many of our cases where the obstacles are hidden deeply in the subconscious mind, this time the issue was right up on the surface, visible to everyone who knew her, and easy to detect.

The cyclic pattern portion of her issues was easy to determine, but of course, there were underlying emotions that were affecting aspects of her life that weren't so obvious.

In this woman's case she always seemed to be pushing away the men in her life, including men she liked and ones who could potentially have turned into long-term relationships.

Her pattern was one where she would meet a guy, he would be a good man, things would be going along great, and then when the relationship got too close for her comfort level, she would start pushing away.

She would develop major distrust of the man, believing that her new lover was obviously cheating on her or doing something wrong because he was a few minutes late for dinner or didn't answer his cellphone immediately. She would build these minor incidences into full-blown conspiracies, proving the man's infidelity, if not in fact, at least in her own mind.

These constructs were based on past behavior in her life, and had no connection to the actual actions of the man. She had her lover convicted and sentenced in her own mind without bothering to let the truth get in her way.

These were constructs she had learned from her parents, her grandparents, her relatives, all in her past.

She may have heard a story when she was seven years old about some neighbors and assorted acts of infidelity, where people were cheating on each other and did get caught. She might have had a childhood friend whose parents divorced and her friend had to move away, leaving our client alone in the playground, worrying about the horrors her now-absent friend had to endure because of some adulterous act committed by some parent.

Sometimes these constructs are formed just by being a witness to other people's actions that may have been distant from the client being affected some many decades later.

In this specific case, our client did not come from a broken home, or have divorce in her family.

We had to dig really deeply to uncover the root of her issues.

We discovered a very high level of guilt assorted with this situation, along with resentment that had grown over the years, building up degrees of self-punishment in our client.

She was an attractive woman who was able to attract a wide assortment of men into her life, but very early in her relationships the bantering, fights, distrust and thoughts of the man being disloyal would develop.

She would start pushing the men away, causing bewilderment with her lovers who didn't understand why such a loving woman with so much potential for having successful long term relationships would suddenly implode with irrational fears and jealousies.

A simple trip to the store would turn into a test of fidelity, putting the man on the defense, having to explain why he was a few minutes late in returning, with her imagining him cheating on her at every opportunity.

She would pick fights, create conflict, and manifest issues that had no basis in any reality.

She would use sex as weapon, withholding it as a tactic to maintain control over her relationships.

The men in her life would see this as her being mean and spiteful, not understanding the underlying issues of guilt, and feelings of being violated by the sex act, all of which are constructs she held deep in her subconscious.

We also discovered what we call the Love-Money Curse, going back to the days when women would be required to have dowries for marriage, keeping the young women prim and proper, learning the rituals and dances for society approval.

The women would have to literally buy their way into the right families, bringing wealth and assets to the exchange and mergers of the day.

Sometimes love was involved, but many times, it was strictly a business transaction, designed to preserve and enhance the fortunes of the various dynasties benefiting from the arranged relationships.

The pressure to dress the right way, have the right appearance, attend the right dances, and say the right things in polite conversations was extremely high.

The expectations on these women were very high and stressful.

You might ask what any of these actions from centuries gone by have to do with our clients of today?

It is a genetic energy built up over the decades, and our client had these generational themes carried over from her grandparents and parents where she was thinking that men had to act a certain way and she had to respond in kind to those actions.

She was projecting her thoughts on to the men in her life, and the men simply couldn't live up to her expectations.

She created impossible situations, and the results were just as predictable. She pushed and pushed, and the men had no choice but to react to her lack of logic.

Using our muscle testing techniques we were able to determine that she equated love with money, a fact that doomed her relationships before they even had a chance to blossom.

These deep subconscious thoughts controlled her comfort level with men and had long-lasting influence on her conscious thoughts and actions.

When asked if men were trustworthy, her muscle testing confirmed her belief that she didn't believe she could trust men on even the most basic level.

This was a huge issue in her ability to have successful relationships, and it didn't really have anything to do with the specific men in her life.

The depth of her underlying patterns was so profound that it was crippling her health and mental state.

She could easily have gone through her entire life without ever finding true love, completely unaware of the real reasons for her discontentment.

If this story rings true for you, or you have friends or family facing similar issues, know that there is hope out there through our work at Shifting Lives, where we offer permanent release for your negative beliefs.

Compassion For Another Person

We had a client in her mid-40s with a great career, a nice house, enjoying all of the comforts of a successful lifestyle, except for the fact that she was single and didn't want to be. While some people are single by choice, preferring the solitary environment, this client ached to be successfully involved romantically with a man.

She had been in an out of a few relationships, including several that had the promise of turning into something lasting and meaningful, but for some reason they never developed beyond the initial flourishes.

We moved on into her story, painting a picture in broad strokes on the canvas of her life, just to see where things were going.

We were looking for themes and cyclic patterns that were causing problems in her life, affecting her emotions and actions.

Very quickly, we discovered an interesting scenario in her life, dealing with her brother, who had been injured while serving his nation in the Vietnam War.

Our client, a kind and caring woman had taken it on herself to take care of her wounded brother, going so far as to literally move next door to her sibling in order to nurse and comfort him.

Meanwhile, she made token efforts to have a normal life of her own, developing numerous relationships over the years, while caring for her brother's daily needs.

In an amazing series of coincidences, every time she would start taking her relationships with men to a more intimate level, something would happen to her brother's health. He would suffer relapses or develop new problems, and my client's promising romances would have to take the back seat while she focused on her number one priority of caring for her wounded hero.

Her days would be filled with going to doctor appointments, running errands, and meeting the needs of her family obligations.

Her romances would wither and die.

Then her brother would recover, and stabilize.

Their lives would go back to what they considered normal.

My client would meet a new man. A budding relationship would ensue, offering the promise of a lasting, loving companionship.

Then her brother's health would deteriorate, a series of medical emergencies would arise, and the cycle would repeat itself.

Her brother would get all of my client's attention, and her relationship would falter and literally disappear.

Once we identified these patterns, our goal was to help our client.

We don't treat conditions.

We weren't hired to treat her brother.

Our focus was on our client and her needs.

The brother was just one of the actors on her stage, where our client created her world from her subconscious mind.

Our client's compassion for her brother was keeping her from sharing her love with any other man, sabotaging her chances for romance and possibly, marriage for herself.

This issue ran deep in her life, even preceding her brother's injuries in Vietnam. Our client had been the caregiver in her family since her childhood, constantly helping her brother with homework, school papers, and more. She had been in the caretaker mode for so long, she couldn't imagine life any other way.

We discovered issues of guilt and fear of abandonment wrapped up in her feelings of compassion for her brother.

When we released all of her fears and constructs, she was able to take what was then a very casual relationship with a new friend, and allowed it to develop into a successful romantic coupling.

It was during this same time period that her brother independently decided to move to a new area, and start his life over with a change of scenery and attitudes.

His sister's new relationship and outlook gave him the strength he needed to start anew in his own life, working to develop meaningful relationships with people outside of his own inner circle.

The latest update on our client is talk of marriage, and her feeling that the vicious cycle that had held her captive was finally over.

All of the passionate energy she had previously devoted to helping her wounded brother was now available for her own needs and desires.

The results were truly life-changing.

---*Review*---

Relationships may very well be our greatest teacher.

Though we have included several stories containing various dramatic scenarios, we will still explain through the Shifting Lives Method's viewpoint as to the motivating factors in these examples.

Emotions involved are "control, anger, abandonment, low self-esteem/worth, unloved and grief."

This chapter is the strongest example of the mirror reflecting back to us, revealing the aspects of self that are crying out to be exposed, then healed.

Shifting Lives Method targets and identifies the age of occurrence, the people involved, the emotion and aspects of life in the experience. Each relationship in our lives is of utmost importance. [This concept will be discussed at length in Chapter 7] Down to the least important encounter with another person, the attitude, energy, actions and expressions are each a vital link back to our most precious relationships. However we act in the least of our encounters with others, it affects the primary relationships we cherish most.

Control is a destructive action at the very core of its energy. The earth itself is a control mechanism, constantly presenting us with opportunity to release attachment to control. Moving into allowance is the answer, and releasing control. You've most certainly heard it said "let go and let God."

Strength comes to you in full force once the grip of control is conquered. Do not let the word conquered throw you.

Releasing the grip of control is not obtained by some forceful move, tincture or mystical herb. It is achieved with awareness, discipline and observation of your every thought, deed and action. The true test is in your interpersonal relationships. Allow relationships to be your guide through this greatest adventure of life.

When it comes to Anger most will agree that social constructs and laws help us keep our anger in check, at least for the most part. Yet, look at anger when it comes to interacting with the ones closest to us. Isn't it more likely that anger is expressed in the safety of our own closest relationships? Therefore discipline, restraint and true compassion must be drawn upon to conquer this deep-seated primal emotion.

"Abandoned" has previously been discussed in earlier chapters, so we will be brief in this example. Abandoned shows itself in the relationship equation in the form of fear, jealousy, and lack of trust, often causing one to push away an otherwise wonderful relationship.

Low self-esteem places us into the lives of people that we would not under ordinary circumstances get involved with. How often is it reported that a prominent member of society losses one of their promising children to the seedy underworld of drugs and crime? In love relationships low self-esteem can cause one to make horrible, even deadly choices with it comes to mate selection.

Unloved usually occurs in early infancy. For the sake of this work unloved is a condition, a state of being, sometimes referred to as a broken heart.

Often mother is the first person creating this condition, unwittingly of course. It can begin with something as simple as a missed or delayed meal or insufficient quantity of a meal. Delayed response to a cry can also be the action of cause generating the feeling of being unloved.

Grief is that deep sense of loss we feel when someone near and dear to us is gone. How then can this emotion effect love relationships? Unresolved grief is often carried as energy of sadness, remaining subtle in nature. Stuffed down inside of one's deep recesses, grief produces an impatience of sorts, and a sadness that creeps into a conversation unexpectedly.

The point of damage to love relationships can be seen as placing blame onto one's partner for not being understanding when sadness arises.

Sympathy is not a cure for unexpressed grief.

We have found two of the main contributing factors responsible for the breakdown of love relationships are "impatience and intolerance."

The fear of death is more to be dreaded than death itself.

~ Pubilius Sirus ~

Chapter Six

Death and Suicide

Surrounded by Suicide

One of the constant facts of my work is I never know what set of issues is going to come into my office on any given day.

A lady needed my help for a very unusual set of patterns that had occurred in her life, starting when she was a very young child.

Our Shifting Lives Method determined that her life was being controlled by the fact that over and over people close to her committed suicide.

It almost sounds like a story made up by an imaginative author, but unfortunately for my client, the facts were all too real.

When my client was at a very, very young age, one of her close relatives committed suicide, having profound effects on the family.

A few years after that, another close family member ended her own life, once again, deeply impacting my client, who was then a young child.

Now you might think the odds of this, while rare, aren't impossible. Things like this, unfortunately, do happen, and maybe the second suicide had something to do with the first act, seeing as how the victims were related.

I agree with this line of reasoning, chalking it up to just a sad and tragic set of occurrences.

What I couldn't explain as easily was when she revealed that a worker, a handyman in her family home, also committed suicide in front of my then-young client with a weapon that was in the house at the time.

While it seems like a scene from an Alfred Hitchcock movie, it was actually signs of a pattern that was crippling my now-adult client.

By her mid-teens, a fourth suicide had happened around my client.

Moving ahead to when my client was in her early-twenties, she found herself at work one day when an armed man came into her building and killed himself in front of dozens of workers,

To top it off, my client married a man whose parent had also killed herself.

My client was literally surrounded by suicide on all sides.

I took her back to her subconscious and found all of these patterns of death around her.

These patterns had her believing that people were unreliable, and that everybody abandoned her.

These beliefs were deeply etched into her mind, causing her to attract the circumstances that her subconscious most needed to see, and heal in her life.

Consider it this way: all of the people around us are actors on our stage. We are the directors. We are the writers. We are the casting agents.

We bring in all of these people to be there on our stage, and we are going to want to look at the things that are going to heal us.

For this client, we were looking at energies of abandonment and issues of control.

Once we started clearing these issues, we saw her life open up, take shape, and become better and better.

That was the ultimate goal for this woman.

We all want to be healthier, happier, and involved in great relationships.

But her notions that people are unreliable, can't be trusted, and would always leave her would turn into a self-fulfilling prophecy.

Clearing out her energies related to death, she became more hopeful, healthier, and open to positive relationships.

If you are living with similar circumstances, rest assured that the same methods that produced real changes in her life are offered to all of our clients at Shifting Lives.

Men Die

We had a client who came into our office seeking help for what she thought were issues about weight and allergies.

When we did our work on her subconscious mind to see where she was positioned on relationships, money and trust in men, it came out that she was attracted to older gentlemen, men who were often decades older than she was.

Her first husband was a healthy man with a military background. He was a successful business executive in great shape mentally and physically.

One day he goes into the hospital for a series of normal checkups, and instead of having a routine experience, he suddenly dies.

Dead and gone.

My client didn't even have time to make it to the hospital to be with her husband in his final moments on earth.

One day she is happy in her normal routine, going about her life, making plans with her healthy spouse, and the next day she is arranging for his burial and coping with life without him.

Shortly after this, her father suffered a similar experience and died unexpectedly.

Again, my client was left to take care of all of the details dealing with his funeral and his estate.

These things happen. People die every day.

Then she told us about yet a third situation where she got involved with an older man, seventeen years her senior, who was healthy, successful, and full of life's energy. He also had a military background, having been a rather high-ranking officer.

The relationship had been evolving, moving along nicely on the road to a probable marriage.

Then this man was suddenly ill, taken to the hospital, and within a few days, he also was dead and gone.

Was this woman a black widow, somehow involved with the deaths of all of these men in her life?

What was attracting all of this negative energy into her relationships?

Our client had a deep belief that men in authority, men in prominent social positions in her world, would suddenly abandon her in her time of need.

This had developed in her childhood when her grandfather died suddenly, and was reinforced with the passing of each man in her life as she grew up.

Her subconscious was reaching out into the world and pulling in scenarios that fit the script she had playing in her mind.

Her script was that she was always supposed to align herself with dignified men of power, and men who had achieved success in life.

Her subconscious mind was out there looking for these kinds of men, but there was a twist in that those same men were not dependable, and couldn't be there for our client in the long term.

She kept choosing men who would abandon her, going to the extreme point of death.

In our session, she mentioned that she had yet another close friend in business with a similar level of success and achievement who also had just recently died suddenly without any warning.

She was now able to see this pattern in her life and was desperate to know what was causing it to happen to her on such a frequent basis.

By testing her subconscious and going way back into her childhood memories, we found there was a theme that had been literally implanted into her by her mother stating that men were not reliable and could not be trusted.

Her mother told her to never base her income, her stability, her home or her security on any men, a belief that came from her mother's generational beliefs and insecurities.

This thought had been implanted in our client at an early age, and she took it to be an absolute truth, never questioning the words of her own mother.

Our client then spent her entire life directing the actors on her stage, fulfilling her mother's prophecies and doubts, playing the roles her mother scripted so many years earlier.

We were able to release all of her doubts, and help her find her path in life.

She soon found herself in a healthy relationship with a kind man who had built a very successful company, which he had sold, and was living on the fruits of his efforts.

---*Review*---

The emotions involved in these stories are "fear, dread, bad memory, anger, abandonment, and disgust." Remember certain words are used in our work which are convenient for our purposes, but not necessarily the dictionary definition.

Fear is intertwined into several of the emotions that I will detail in this summery, so it needs no in-depth explanation. Bad memory and also abandonment are self explanatory in these cases. Therefore the focus will be on dread and disgust as they pertain to these examples.

Let's begin with "Dread". Dread is an interesting word, meaning to fear greatly, or to be in apprehension of something in the future. It applies in these cases quite similar to the textbook definition.

In the recesses of these clients' subconscious minds was a deep groove, a memory of a wound that created a profound fear of death. As Psychiatrist Carl Jung stated "that which you resist persists," having this intense fear of death manifesting into dread literally brought scenarios of death into these women's lives.

By now you have read many examples showing the power of the subconscious mind to create outward circumstances. Stay with me on this one. Some true learning is just around the corner.

We are the director, casting agent, and writer of our personal play. These two scenarios are perfect examples to help solidify the construct in your thoughts.

How else could a person draw so much death into her life? Placing ourselves into circumstances like this would be impossible without the subconscious desire fueling the passion to face then heal the wounds of dread.

Please consider that paramedics, ER doctors, police officers, and others who surround themselves with death and the opportunities to see death, are most likely also carrying the energy of dread.

In each of these cases the client was not consumed with the fear of dying. They were both afraid of death. What then is the difference?

The fear of death that these women were each experiencing was the dread of life itself. The fear surrounding birth and the difficulties and dangers surrounding the delivery process was the fear.

Each of our clients had deep profound subconscious memories of birth trauma.

However you choose to understand the proceeding examples is up to you. I am reporting that both of these women were in dread over the fear of birth. The memories go back to the womb during conception to birth. Fear of themselves dying or of their mothers dying or both dying during the delivery phase of the birthing process were real and present.

 Both of these women survived their births, as did their mothers, so where did the bad memory, dread, fear and disgust come from?

Subconscious testing revealed in both cases past memories of death during the birthing experience. The subconscious holds memories from generations of lifetimes, whether it is in our DNA or in some past life. It is there, none the less.

Disgust reveals in our work close to the dictionary definition "to cause loathing or nausea in." Disgust shows up as stomach energy felt as a low level discomfort or a twinge. This feeling is often ignored. Some might even think its purpose is a protection device warning us of impending danger. For the sake of our work, disgust is more the memory of past experience. Energy is stored in the stomach area unexpressed waiting for an opportunity to create a scenario in which to make itself known, hopefully for healing.

The aspects of life that are present in these stories are career, relationship, physical body, spiritual, personal power and death.

Part Two

It's Not Them

Here is the test to find whether your mission on earth is finished; if you are alive it isn't.

~ Richard Bach ~

Each of you has your own unique life experience, no more, no less valid than any other person.

What we are going to talk about in the following chapters is how your belief system has shaped the life you are now living.

We want to look at the experiences of the story that you are in. I'm going to show you and offer a solution to your past. Whether the past and the present you are living now are beautiful and joyous or whether the past and present you are living in is a bit of misfortune, I would like to offer you a way to rewrite the past, allowing you a chance to build a better present and future.

Using universal laws I'm going to show you a way to rewrite your past experience.

It's Not Them

It's not them. If anyone has ever been to a talk that I've given in the past, you've heard this. I've had you write it down. I would like for you to become very familiar with the term "It's not them."

The people, places, and events that you're seeing in your life today are the things that you have created out of your own subconscious mind. The scenarios you have attracted to yourself are the ones most needed to reveal the areas that need healing.

It is very easy to blame others. It seems to be the way of our world today. We've learned it through television, and through our court system. We always want to know who is guilty and who is innocent. Whose fault is it? It is just the way society has structured itself in our world as we know it today.

In the next chapter, I will introduce the Components of You. We will discuss the Stages of Development that Professor Robert Kegan from Harvard spent his life working on. We use his work and the work of others, including Abraham Maslow, Erik Erickson, B.F. Skinner, Albert Ellis, John Diamond, and Ken Wilber.

Shifting Lives considers a zero order and a sixth order in the stages of personal development. We also center our work around the subconscious mind, and that's my favorite area.

I am convinced all humans are born with more gifts than we know. Most are born geniuses and just get de-geniused rapidly.

~ Buckminister Fuller ~

Chapter Seven

Harmonic You & Your Component Parts

As human beings, we are many different component parts. We are made up of the physical aspects of ourselves. Within the physical, we have an emotional and mental part of ourselves, our spiritual lives, relationships, and careers.

The Physical Health

We are finely-tuned organic beings with systems and components. It's important for us to be aware of each component part, and take control of ourselves. Understand that each of the different parts of ourselves are important. You know one hand is no more important than the other, one foot is no more important that the other. We are a complete system, a whole component part of ourselves.

I encourage everyone to consider a healthy diet. Look at the food that you are eating, the things you're doing to yourself, because it's all very important to the physical part of us. With all of the popular focus on whole foods, fresh vegetables, organic produce, less trans-fats, choose a diet that reflects your lifestyle.

Moderate exercise is good for us. Do it. Do something. Find some form of exercise that is enjoyable, even if it's just simply walking, being out in the fresh air and opening yourselves up to that. Create time in your day to allow for self-caring.

Allow yourself to live in a safe environment, having good shelter, and drinking good clean water. Giving attention to all of these aspects is important to our whole state of being.

Our body is an outward expression of our inner state of being. That's the part I want you to hang on to. Whatever you are seeing in your physical body is an outward expression of your conscious and subconscious mind.

Emotional Well Being

Our emotional state ranges from simple and joyous types of expression to being sad and hurt. Somewhere around 30% of all people today are on some sort of mood altering substance. That is an amazing fact. It seems difficult to imagine that being a true statistic.

Antidepressant use is up 234% in the United Kingdom.

France has doubled its use of antidepressants, as has British Columbia.

The U.S. increased from 13 million prescriptions in 1996 to 27 million in 2005. Even worse, in 2008, more than 164 million prescriptions were written.

Between 30% and 50% of all people taking antidepressants show no response. As if that were not bad enough SSRI side effects include nausea, diarrhea, agitation, headaches and sexual dysfunction. Isn't that enough to cause depression? Suicide rates double while on antidepressants. Clinical evidence and pharmaceutical reasoning state "SSRI drugs blunt your ability to fall in love and stay in love."

The problem of depression is not solved by the use of pharmaceutical drugs when the issue is in the subconscious mind.

Things that affect us emotionally during our developmental years are appearances, things that we look at out in the world and see. Then we develop some type of feeling or expression about it.

I use this story as an example. When you are young, you walk out of your house into the front yard. Out of nowhere a little brown dog runs up and bites you on the ankle. You now have a choice at that point; do you begin to dislike dogs completely, thinking to yourself, "oh my god, I see a dog, and it is going to bite me?" Or do you just become selective and say, "I dislike brown dogs because a brown dog came up and bit me?"

There is even another possibility. You can just be the witness observing someone else get bitten by the little brown dog, and still develop a fear, a phobia, about dogs.

Another possible choice you can make is that it was just a random event. You may think, "A little brown dog came up and bit me. So what, it's no big deal. It doesn't affect me or my subconscious mind at all."

We all develop our emotional state through a series of choices. We develop it through thousands of experiences based on appearances viewed through our own unique set of filters.

The other view is an evidence-based experience, and an example that most people can grasp is when the Surgeon General puts a warning on a certain things and says "cigarette smoking is harmful to your health." We assume that is a true statement that comes from a governmental organization. The Surgeon General is supposedly the top doctor in the country, and we just assume that that his statement is true.

So in our life and in our life experiences, it is easy to take this evidence and say "I'll make that part of my life, because it seems to be true." Then we all develop and give it the weight and power we choose to.

As for the emotional state, I encourage you to consider this statement, "We are influenced by circumstances, but not dictated by them."

Mental Health

The frontal lobe portion of our brain is our personality and thinking facility. I believe that our conscious mind is born when we are born, and it dies when we die. And that is why our personality is a certain way. We, as young, developing individuals do go through this modeling experience.

I definitely work with and believe the John B. Watson Modeling Behavior Theory. Watson had a very famous concept that he told many people, basically stating that he could take a pair of healthy infants, and can turn one into being a common laborer, and the other into being a board certified neurosurgeon."

 He would accomplish this by giving each of the boys certain tasks, circumstances and life situations which would develop one into a person who follows orders and works well with his hands, and one into a skillful person who can read, go in depth, do research and study, and be very skilled. Modeling creates behaviors by giving a child certain types of experiences, created and developed through stages.

The cerebral cortex is the portion of the brain that houses our subconscious. I call it the "Seat of the Soul." We believe that if there is an altar or temple inside our body, it sits in this cerebral cortex, where the subconscious mind exists and rests. There is a timeless portion of us which is shaped over eons of time, and that is our subconscious mind.

We are complex beings, and we are hopefully all on the path of self-discovery. We pick up certain religious views as we go along on our lives. Some of the things we want to take a look at are the key components to spiritual awareness, acceptance and allowance. Those words all happen to start with A, so I guess we can call those The Three A's.

There have been many very wise teachers that have told us to love our neighbors as ourselves, and I think that is very important. This belief is something we should spend a lot of time with. Because if you are going to love others, you have to love yourself before you can truly love something outside of yourself.

I think we should spend a lot of energy, a lot of time developing self-love.

You should also judge not, lest you be judged.

Why would we be interested in that? What would that mean to us?

Whenever you are placing judgment on something outside of yourself, remember "It's not them." That same measure of judgment is going to come back to us. It is best not to do it, or you will have to deal with the circumstances. You know in the old portion of the Bible scriptures the Torah said "and eye for an eye, a tooth for a tooth," which sounded kind of harsh.

The courts used a modified version of this teaching as a foundation for our law system. Another point of view is love is the fulfillment of the law. From our point of view, the subconscious point of view, I believe that we will receive a larger measure in return than the energy we give out.

"What goes around comes around," is very true.

When you are giving out love and kindness, peace, joy and happiness, those things have a tendency to come back to you.

When you are giving out anger and rage, spitefulness and resentment, those things are going to come right back to you.

There is a time lag between our actions and the measurable results, therefore we do not see the immediate repercussions from our misdeeds.

Take a teenager who might be interested in stealing something off of someone's car. He goes in late at night, creeps around and finds this thing he wants. He takes it off of the car, and he gets away with it.

He doesn't get caught.

He doesn't get arrested.

No one saw him do it.

Then ten days later, he's playing basketball with some friends and breaks his ankle.

He is not going to say, "huh, maybe I broke my ankle because I stole parts off of someone's car." But it is interesting to think about that, and to ponder if things like that are possible?

Does the subconscious mind build up guilt? Does it build up resentment against ourselves and then punish us?

Read on to find out how our actions affect our daily lives.

Relationships

Every relationship we are involved in is critically important to the very foundation of our lives. By relationships, we include more than family, not just mom, dad, siblings, spouses, and extended families. Let us look deeper and start thinking about all of the people who are in your life. This will include your co-workers, your colleagues, your friends, and people that are outside of your inner circle.

We have a relationship with people who come into our homes to work on our heating and air system, a plumber, or anyone who does any kind of task for you. Some of you are fortunate enough to have someone who comes and mows your yard. But even deeper still, if you start thinking about all of the people you interact with in just a day's time, the cashier at the super market, the waitress, the clerk…the list keeps on growing. These are people you might not think about having a relationship with, but you do.

Every relationship that you are in affects all of the others. If you have something you are not congruent with in the least of your relationships, it will trickle up and affect your relationship with your spouse, your parents, and your family. There is a direct correlation to each and every person in your life.

We are a system of component parts, not just one little part where one thing has no affect on the other.

In a sense, we are a lot like a computer. If your computer has one little issue, maybe it deals with the video bus that carries information, then your computer is not going to work very well. Just one small piece, a very small component is at fault, yet it will affect the whole.

I would like for you to remember "It's not them."

I'd like for you to remember that we are made up of component parts. We are many different parts of something that we see as being one being. So just the tiniest aspect can be a key element in the functioning of the whole you.

There was this saying about "Don't worry about the speck that is in your brother's eye, until you remove the large particle that is in your own." That is so true and meaningful if you really think about it. How is it that we really have the right to judge someone or to make judgments of another person unless we have really looked closely at ourselves? We really need to examine ourselves, by stating "Gosh I have this little issue going on within me that I need to check on and clear out."

We can only love someone else as much as we love ourselves.

Career

Your career and contributions to society is our next focus. This is such an individual choice, with every one doing their own thing. Consider the cooperative view of business interaction, where we are working with our fellow humans for the good of all, rather than the competitive side. Rather than beat, or outdo our neighbor for our own self-interest, let us work in harmony with one another. I just hope that each one of you have found something that you can do that you love, enjoy, and that brings you happiness and fulfillment. Hopefully, your actions will contribute to society; if for no other reason than it builds character and makes us feel good about ourselves.

Obviously there are additional considerations like finances, contributions to society, sports and recreation, education, and others that help make up a person's whole being, the component parts of you.

Life is a process of becoming, a combination of states we have to go through where people fail if they wish to elect one state and remain in it. This is a kind of death.

~ Anais Nin ~

Chapter Eight

Stages of Personal Development

The intent of this chapter is to bring light to various points of view, theories, models and methods described by many of the world's greatest thinkers.

How the human consciousness is formed? What are the influences that shape and create our lives? What are the issues, experiences and circumstances that make you – you?

We have several greats to consider; Abraham Maslow presenting hierarchy of needs, Erik Erickson, a student of Sigmund Freud with his psychosocial stages of development, B.F. Skinner with Behaviorism, and Robert Kegan's orders of development. We will also consider the primer of Freud's theory as presented by Calvin S. Hall, Carl Jung's archetypes, Ken Wilber's AQAL quadrants, John Diamond's tenets on behavior and finally, Albert Ellis with Rational Emotive Behavior Therapy. Each of these theories, models and tenets will be explained in a brief summary as it is related to our Shifting Lives Method.

Abraham Maslow

Maslow's hierarchy of needs can best be explained by viewing his pyramid of needs.

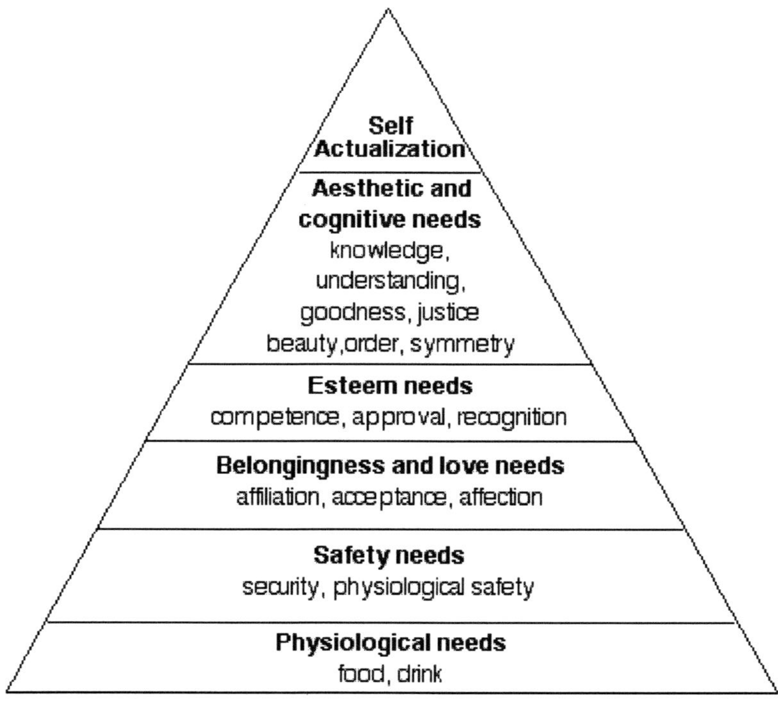

Maslow was interested in the motivations of human behavior, the driving forces behind action. His theory stated there are five layers of needs for all humans: physiological, safety, social, esteem, and the crowning jewel, self-actualization. Maslow attempted to formulate a needs-based framework of human motivation, based upon his clinical experiences with humans, rather than prior psychology theories of his day from leaders in the field of psychology such as Freud and B.F. Skinner, which were largely theoretical or based upon animal behavior.

Erik Erikson

Erikson's psychosocial stages of development are best explained with this chart.

Stage	Basic Conflict	Important Events	Outcome
Infancy (birth to 18 months)	Trust vs. Mistrust	Feeding	Children develop a sense of trust when caregivers provide reliability, care, and affection. A lack of this will lead to mistrust.
Early Childhood (2 to 3 years)	Autonomy vs. Shame and Doubt	Toilet Training	Children need to develop a sense of personal control over physical skills

Early Childhood Continued			and a sense of independence. Success leads to feelings of autonomy, failure results in feelings of shame and doubt.
Preschool (3 to 5 years)	Initiative vs. Guilt	Exploration	Children need to begin asserting control and power over the environment. Success in this stage leads to a sense of purpose. Children who try to exert too much power experience disapproval, resulting in a sense of guilt.
School Age (6 to 11 years)	Industry vs. Inferiority	School	Children need to cope with new social and academic demands. Success leads to a sense of competence, while failure results in feelings of inferiority.
Adolescence (12 to 18 years)	Identity vs. Role Confusion	Social Relationships	Teens need to develop a sense of self and personal identity. Success leads to an ability to stay true to self, while failure leads to role confusion and a weak sense of self.
Young Adulthood (19 to 40 years)	Intimacy vs. Isolation	Relationships	Young adults need to form intimate, loving relationships with other people. Success leads to

Young Adulthood	Continued		strong relationships, while failure results in loneliness and isolation.
Middle Adulthood (40 to 65 years)	Generatively vs. Stagnation	Work and Parenthood	Adults need to create or nurture things that will outlast them, often by having children or creating a positive change that benefits other people. Success leads to feelings of usefulness and accomplishment, while failure results in shallow involvement in the world.
Maturity (65 to death)	Ego Integrity vs. Despair	Reflection on Life	Older adults need to look back on life and feel a sense of fulfillment. Success at this stage leads to feelings of wisdom, while failure results in regret, bitterness, and despair.

B. F. Skinner

B.F. Skinner coined the term Behaviorism believing that learning is a function of change in response to stimuli that occur in our environment. By way of example, consider the implications of reinforcement theory as applied to the development of programmed instruction (Markle, 1969; Skinner, 1968)

1. Practice should take the form of question (stimulus) - answer (response) frames which expose the student to the subject in gradual steps

2. Require that the learner make a response for every frame and receive immediate feedback

3. Try to arrange the difficulty of the questions so the response is always correct and hence a positive reinforcement

4. Ensure that good performance in the lesson is paired with secondary rein-forcers such as verbal praise, prizes and good grades.

Principles:

1. Behavior that is positively reinforced will reoccur; intermittent reinforcement is particularly effective

2. Information should be presented in small amounts so that responses can be reinforced ("shaping")

3. Reinforcements will generalize across similar stimuli ("stimulus generalization") producing secondary conditioning

John Diamond

It is difficult for us to truly know our mother's love. One main reason is connected with our brain's misprocessing – a consequence of uncorrected birthing trauma caused by the difficulty of our present evolutionary state: too large a fetal head and too small a maternal pelvis (Wills, 1993). The school of cranial osteopathy contends that the uncorrected physical distortions of the body, especially of the skull bones, as a result of the birthing process are the cause of so many of our later structural and therefore physiological problems. Dr. Diamond not only agrees with this, but adds that it is this birthing trauma which is the predominant cause of all of our emotional and spiritual difficulties, hence of our anguish.

This misprocessing affects us and our inability to receive our mother's love and it affects our mother, who as the result of the trauma of her own birth hinders her ability to fully manifest her innate Maternal Instinct.

The task of our lives may be seen as the overcoming of our misprocessing so as to then see past our mother's own misprocessing to the Mother she yearned to be.

Only then will we be in touch with the higher truth that our mother, and therefore the world, loves us always. Thus the very basis of Dr. Diamond's work, of his philosophy, as a minister of souls, is to help you overcome the impediments of your birthing trauma, your misprocessing so that your anguish may be diminished, and you will hopefully live a high Life Energy life of Belovedness and Cantillation. That is what makes Dr. Diamond's work—his philosophy— truly unique.

The Philosophy of Positive Health

Five of the primary tenets upon which Dr. Diamond's approach to positive health rest are:

1.The critical importance of the reduction of stress and the balancing of the concomitant emotional attitudes. Disease is seen as arising from stress that causes a general reduction in Life Energy and specific energy imbalances throughout the body.

2.The essential role of primary prevention — prevention before pathological change, either mental or physical. At this early stage the energy imbalances may be described as fluid or dynamic and readily amenable to correction. If the stress is prevented, if the mental attitudes are changed, then primary prevention will be possible.

3.The individual's responsibility for taking charge of his own health and his own way through life. In this context the role of the so-called doctor is that of teacher — to explain and to help the individual to see exactly what he is doing to lower his own healing energies. The individual has superimposed maladaptive behavioral patterns upon himself which have pulled him away from his natural, "normal" state, and he must recognize and alter them.

4.That great healing forces exist within us and in nature to enable repair to occur once the stress is reduced and the negative attitudes are corrected. It is recognized that natural methods are essential since unnatural methods often diminish Life Energy. While these unnatural methods may provide symptomatic relief, they ultimately lower the Life Energy, retard the true healing process, and ignore the stress and the attitudinal problems that are at the base of the disease patterns.

5.That most problems begin at an energy level. The first physical manifestation of imbalance within the body is at an energy level and corrections can be made at this level. On top of this are the metabolic, environmental, structural and nutritional problems that also require attention.

When a man is perfect in his own nature, body, and soul, perfect in his harmonious adaptations and action, and living in perfect harmony with nature, with his fellowman and with God, he may be said to be in a state of Health. The broad philosophy of Life Energy enhancement includes as a goal the achievement of positive health. To assist in achieving this, one is taught the insights and understandings and the methods of preventive medicine, including nutrition, psychological insights, bioharmonics, and psycho-aesthetics. Psychoaesthetics is a field of work in which Dr. Diamond has developed techniques for assessing the effects of works of art, poetry, music, architecture, craftsmanship, body movement and dance, gesture and posture on the physical, mental and emotional functioning of the individual. In addition, there are techniques for stress reduction via the aesthetic experience.

Ken Wilber

AQAL: "All Quadrants All Levels" represents the core of Wilber's work. AQAL stands for "all quadrants all levels", but equally connotes 'all lines', 'all states' and 'all types'. These are the five irreducible categories of Wilber's model of manifest existence.

All of Wilber's AQAL categories—quadrants, lines, levels, states, and types—relate to relative truth in the two truths doctrine of Buddhism, to which he subscribes. According to Wilber, none of them are true in an absolute sense: only formless awareness, "the simple feeling of being," exists absolutely.
An account or theory is said to be AQAL, and thus integral (inclusive or comprehensive), if it accounts for or makes reference to all four quadrants and four major levels in Wilber's ontological scheme. AQAL system

138

has been critiqued for not taking into account the lack of change in the biological structure of the brain at the human level, this role being taken instead by human-made artifacts.

Quadrants

<table>
<tr><td>Upper-Left
(UL)</td><td>Upper-Right
(UR)</td></tr>
<tr><td>"I"
Interior Individual
Intentional

e.g. Freud</td><td>"It"
Exterior Individual
Behavioral

e.g. Skinner</td></tr>
<tr><td>Lower-Left
(LL)</td><td>Lower-Right
(LR)</td></tr>
<tr><td>"We"
Interior Collective
Cultural

e.g. Gadamer</td><td>"Its"
Exterior Collective
Social

e.g. Marx</td></tr>
</table>

Each holon, or unit of reality that is both a whole and a part of a larger whole, has an interior and an exterior. It also exists as an individual and (assuming more than one of these entities exists) as a collective. Observing the holon from the outside constitutes an exterior perspective on that holon. Observing it from the inside is the interior perspective, and so forth. If you map these four perspectives into quadrants, you have four quadrants, or dimensions

To give an example of how this works, consider four schools of social science. Freudian psychoanalysis, which interprets people's interior experiences, is an account of the interior individual (or, in the diagram, the upper-left) quadrant. B. F. Skinner's behaviorism, which limits itself to the observation of the behavior of organisms, is an exterior individual (upper-right) account. Gadamer's philosophical hermeneutics interprets the collective consciousness of a society, and is thus an interior plural (lower-left) perspective. Marxist economic theory, according to Wilber, examines the external behavior of a society (lower-right).

All four pursuits – psychoanalysis, behaviorism, philosophical hermeneutics and Marxism – offer complementary, rather than contradictory, perspectives. It is possible for all to be correct and necessary for a complete account of human existence.

Also, each by itself offers only a partial view of reality. On his view, Wilber has integrated these four areas of knowledge through an acknowledgement of the four fundamental dimensions of existence. Further, according to Wilber, these four perspectives are equally valid at all levels of existence.
According to Wilber, all holons have multiple lines of development, or intelligences—in fact, over two dozen have been observed. They include cognitive, ethical,

aesthetic, spiritual, kinesthetic, affective, musical, spatial, logical-mathematical, karmic, etc. One can be highly developed cognitively (cerebrally smart) without being highly morally developed (as in the case of Nazi doctors). However, Wilber acknowledges, you cannot be highly morally developed without the pre-requisite cognitive development. So not all of the developmental lines are ontologically equivalent.

Levels or stages

The concept of levels follows closely on the concept of lines of development. The more highly developed you are in a particular line, the higher level you are at in that line. Wilber's conception of the level is clearly based on several theories of developmental psychology, including: Piaget's theory of cognitive development, Kohlberg's stages of moral development, Maslow's hierarchy of needs, Erikson's stages of psychosocial development, and Jane Loevinger's stages of ego development.

The exceptional feature of Wilber's approach is that, under this methodology, all of these mental structures—subconscious, rational, mystical—are considered complementary and legitimate, rather than competing in a zero-sum conceptual space. And that is perhaps Wilber's greatest accomplishment—the opening up of a space wherein more ideas, theories, beliefs, and stories can be considered true, responsible, and acceptable.

Many criticize the strict hierarchical nature of Wilber's conception of the level in psychological and cultural development, which he compares to the hierarchical nature of matter itself. Sub-atomic particles are composed of quarks. Atoms are made of sub-atomic particles. Molecules are made of atoms. Cell organelles are made of molecules, etc. One must attain the lower levels before the higher levels because the higher levels are constituted by the lower level components. Thus, when represented graphically, the levels should appear as concentric circles, with higher levels transcending but also including lower ones. Wilber also attacks the equating of hierarchy with patriarchy using a similar line of argument.

States

States refer to those aspects of consciousness that are temporal, passing, experiential, and phenomenal. Wilber's later works develop close relations between states and levels/lines (or structures) but the relations between these two major aspects of consciousness are often misconstrued. The misunderstanding is based on the idea that a person can "peak experience" a higher structure which, as Wilber has said, would be like a first year piano student playing for a moment like a seasoned virtuoso. Even though the vocabulary (subtle, causal, nondual) of states and of higher structures is similar, higher states do not equate with higher structures. Wilber's mantra to quell this misunderstanding is: "States are free but structures are earned." One has to build or earn structure, it can't be peak experienced for free.

Theory of Truth

Wilber argues that manifest reality is composed of four domains, and that each domain, or "quadrant" has its own truth-standard, or test for validity, as follows:

	Interior	Exterior
Individual	Standard: Truthfulness (1st person) (sincerity, integrity, trustworthiness)	Standard: Truth (3rd person) (correspondence, representation, propositional)
Collective	Standard: Justness (2nd person) (cultural fit, rightness, mutual understanding)	Standard: Functional fit (3rd person) (systems theory web, structural-functionalism, social systems mesh)

Interior individual/1st person - "If we look at the actual interior of an individual [entity], then we have an entirely different type of validity claim. The question here is not, is it raining outside? The question here is, When I tell you it is raining outside, am I telling you the truth or am I lying? You see, here it is not so much a question of whether the map matches the objective territory, but whether the mapmaker can be trusted. You can always check and see if it's raining. Interior events are located in states of consciousness, not in objective states of affairs, and so you can't empirically nail them down with simple consensus location. "I might lie to you. I might lie to myself. I might misrepresent and not know it."

Interior collective/2nd person - "The subjective world is situated in an intersubjective space, a cultural space without this cultural background. I wouldn't have the tools to interpret my own thoughts to myself. So here the validity claim is not so much objective propositional truth, or subjective truthfulness, but intersubjective fit. This cultural background provides the common context against which my own interior thoughts and beliefs will have some sort of meaning, and so the validity criteria here involves the "cultural fit" [of a statement] within this background. What is so remarkable about common understanding is not that I can take a simple word like "dog" and point to a real dog and say "I mean that." What is so remarkable is that you know what I mean by that. [So it is] a matter of how we arrange collectively, our ethics, morals, laws, culture, group or collective identities, background contexts."

Exterior individual/3rd person - "We check to see if the proposition corresponds with or fits the facts, if the map accurately reflects the real [exterior] territory, if we cannot disprove it we may assume it is accurate enough. But the essential idea is that my statement somehow refers to an objective state of affairs, and it fairly accurately somehow corresponds with those objects or processes or affairs. All of which is fair enough and important enough, and I in no way deny the general importance of empirical representation. It's just not the whole story."

Exterior collective/3rd person - "The main validity claim is functional fit, how entities fit together in a system. So in systems theory you will find nothing about ethical standards, values, morals, mutual understanding, truthfulness, sincerity, depth, integrity, aesthetics. It describes the system in purely objective exterior terms, from without. It doesn't want to know how collective values are intersubjectively shared in mutual understanding. Rather, it looks at how their objective correlates functionally fit in the overall system.

All four of these are valid forms of knowledge, because they are grounded in the realities of the nature of every holon. And therefore all four of these truth claims can be confirmed or rejected by a community of the adequate [those competent in that knowledge]. They each have a different validity claim which carefully guides us, through checks and balances, on our knowledge quest. They are all falsifiable within their own domains, which means false claims can be dislodged by further evidence."

Robert Kegan

There are five stages of development, according to Professor Robert Kegan from Harvard University. He is the one who really popularized this concept, but there are a lot of psychologists and professors out in the community that work with this model.

Conception to Birth

Some say that traditional psychology leaves off the first order: conception to birth.

I think that conception to birth is a very important part of our development. In the womb, we are hearing things that are around us. We are experiencing life through our mothers. We are experiencing the tone. We are experiencing vibration. We are interacting with our mother, through her feelings, her hormones and the different energetic parts that can move through that blood placenta barrier into the developing fetus.

If any of you reading this are pregnant, or involved with a pregnant woman's life, you might share this information with them and reiterate the importance of being kind, being joyous, being loving, and playing soft music. That was very popular for a while, the concept of exposing fetuses to the works of Beethoven, Bach, and other varieties of soft music. Just exposing the developing fetus to positive things like good vibrations takes advantage of this line of thought, allowing a lot of invention and influences to come through there.

The next one is called the magical mind state.

It's generally considered between 0-7 years. I personally think the strongest development of that is really from birth to five years of age.

We start to identify ourselves separately once we are above the age of five. What is unique about this, this magical mind, this first order, is we don't have a good size and spatial relationship when we are very, very young.

We see examples of this in some children when they may look up, and see an airplane. It is a Boeing 747 but yet they think it is about as big as their own tiny fingers. And it is to them, because they can look up there, hold up their fingers and conclude that is about how big an airplane is.

Later they will go to the airport to pick someone up and they will see all these people coming off this plane. In their minds they just don't get how that is even possible for the plane to be that big.

They go to the window, see this enormous plane, and still don't put the two things together.

"Oh, the plane I saw up in the sky was 30,000 ft. in the air, 5 or 6 miles away and it was only as big as my fingers, but the one right here is so much larger."

Here is another interesting thing that we actually found in one of our sessions. Some of us were bathed in a sink when we were little, and mom would be bathing us. At the end she would pull the stopper and water would start running down the drain. When you are in this magic mind state of your being you see the soap bubble, whirling around the sink and "whoop" down the drain it goes. Well, in our little undeveloped conscious state we go, "oh my god, I'm next."

You literally think you're going into that drain. Maybe you think that you don't really remember back that far. But you do. These are things that we found in our work back in the subconscious. That is why some babies are frantic during a bath. They don't want to go down the drain. So it is all about time, space and relationship to size.

Instrumental Mind

The next stage is called the instrumental mind.

This is generally considered to be from age seven into adolescence, but it can actually go into adulthood.

A lot of people get stuck in this phase.

In the instrumental mind objects do stay the same size, and you start learning that no matter what their distance or relationship is to you, the objects remain set and solid.

But here is one of the interesting parts to us. Rules are not broken during this phase due to the fear of getting caught. One of the things we develop, usually after age seven, once we gain an identity of self, we start not wanting to break the rules, knowing there are consequences for getting caught. Some people grow out of that later, but that is not the norm.

You tend to not lie to other people due to the fear of retaliation. And in this stage we tend to look at people, say our friends particularly, as helpers. So if we wanted to do something, we would go to our friends and say "hey, let's get together and go do this thing." But we tend to see teachers and authority figures as barriers to getting what we want. So we are looking at people in this phase as either helpers or barriers.

Socialized Traditional Mind

The next stage is adult; the socialized traditional mind.

People in this order no longer see others as a means to an end, so we generally move someone past that. But we use external authorities to gain confidence to help with our sense of self.

So in this particular order we might find that we have the need for others to validate us, like our bosses, a certain religion, maybe a governmental agency or certain types of clubs. You might have rigid beliefs about government. You might have rigid beliefs about your religion, groups and organization. It often feels like you are torn between two things.

In this stage there's an interesting thing. If you have the opportunity to go to say, a thanksgiving dinner, at your parents' home, or your significant other's home, you might feel really torn between them. You may have a difficult time making that decision because you don't want to disappoint the one, and you don't want to disappoint the wife or husband. So you just feel torn.

In this phase you don't necessarily have good psychological boundaries. We tend to use this type of thinking to justify being able to just intrude into someone's boundaries, so let's move onto a happier one.

Self-authorizing Modern Mind

This is the self-authorizing modern mind.

In this state you learn that your self can exist outside of a relationship of others. You feel connected to your own principles, apart from government, apart from religion, and apart from society. I really see a lot of people fit into this category and see life more this way.

We are not just wound up just because someone told us something or someone is trying to make us do some act.

Unlike the second order, we do take people's suggestions into account, though we end up making our own decision about things. And unlike the third order, we don't have to rely on authority figures.

So this is a good place to be. This is something you should really work towards, finding yourself in this space. And you become really self-motivated. Even if your way of doing things isn't the best or the most complete, you still want to do things your own way.

That's not a negative to this; it's just how we are. When you are deeply into this state, you just see it clearly.

You decide you want to do something, perhaps open a business. Even if the powers that be say it's not the best idea in the world, you still think "I can do it anyway." Because you are thinking on your own, you are not listening to statistics or considering the economy or weighing those types of things. You move yourself outside of that.

Self-transformation

This is self-transformation.

Kegan said 5% of most adults actually get to this phase of self-transformation or post modern mind.

A good example of this would be in the old times, concerning a village elder. This is someone that went beyond just being a tribal person and moved up to being an elder or an authority. It's the people that got to where they are today because they had wisdom about things.

To be in this stage you have learned all there is to learn in the other stages, and you are not limited by your own inner systems. You are looking at the similarities that are hidden inside what used to look like differences, and this is the really important part of this.

I hope you can start seeing this and look at your own life. Look at what your seeing out there. Look at how you are seeing other people. Look at how you see schools, colleges, religions and even governments. See how similar things are; rather than these difference, because it is easy to pick out this one little difference. You know these certain people wear this thing on their head and those other people where that thing on their head, whereas those people stand up and face this way when they pray. Just start looking at what is similar about everything in the world, instead of picking out those little differences.

People in the fifth order are less likely to see themselves with defined traits. They free themselves from strongly defined views about the world and about themselves. That is one of the ways it really differs, especially from the third and fourth orders.

You become increasingly identified with your own consciousness, and you really start dropping off all of your rigid concepts.

You have the ability to see how the privileged and the oppressed work within this world. We had conversations a lot like that at meetings. We were talking about groups of people in society; and if we should run and help someone who seems a little disadvantaged at life or not? It is an interesting choice, and an interesting decision.

Is it our place to get out and fix everything?

In the fifth order you have the ability to take multiple perspectives to identify with other people's outlooks, but then you don't feel torn between those two. You consider many different perspectives, and you see them as apart of yourself. You attempt to create yourself out of this complex nature of reality and universe. You are basically clearly defining yourself but you are also not locking into things outside yourself. You are not limited by beliefs that are merely giving you comfort.

A fifth order person also is more psychologically free than the other orders; so you are not so rigidly attached to constructs. You recognize the developmental nature of human beings, which is also an important part of this. Therefore you know that people are just seeing the world at different levels, different constructs. That would help you understand why we don't always just rush out and help someone; because they are in some phase of their own development.

Sigmund Freud

Sigmund Freud, often referred to as the father of psychology, explored the subconscious mind as the storehouse of causation. Due to the magnitude of Freud's work we will site a primer of his work compiled by Calvin S. Hall

Over and above all of the other virtues of Feud's theory stands this one-it tries to envision full–bodied individuals living partly in a world of reality and partly in a world of make-believe, beset by conflicts and inner contradictions, yet capable of rational thought and action, moved by forces of which they have little knowledge and by aspirations that are beyond their reach, by turn confused and clearheaded, frustrated and satisfied, hopeful and despairing, selfish and altruistic; in short a complex human being. For many people, this picture of the individual has an essential validity (Theories of Personality). Calvin S. Hall 1979

Carl Jung

Carl Jung is noted for stating; "that which you resist ~ persists." Jung considered the process of individualization necessary for a person to become whole. "May each one seek his own way, the way leads to mutual love in community. Men will come to see and feel the similarity and commonality of their ways."

Jung used symbolic components called archetypes not actual persons or objects. Archetype means mould or model in Greek. Jung did not expound on where the archetypes come from though like Freud, Jung believed that memories are collected into the archaic heritage by repetitious experience.

Basic Archetypes: a brief list

The child; wounded child, magical child, divine child

The self; striving to find self realization

The victim; blames others for their life, poor little me

The artist; inspired visionary seeking truth

The shadow; remnant of our animalistic self

"It seems to me that their origin can only be explained by assuming them to be deposits of the constantly repeating experiences of humanity" C. Jung

Albert Ellis

Albert Ellis is our last great mind to consider in this chapter. Ellis is best known for Rational Emotive Behavior Therapy (REBT). The following is the best model by which to view Ellis's life work.

The ABC Model

Albert Ellis and REBT posit that our reaction to having our goals blocked (or even the possibility of having them blocked) is determined by our beliefs. To illustrate this, Dr. Ellis developed a simple ABC format to teach people how their beliefs cause their emotional and behavioral responses:

A. Something happens.
B. You have a belief about the situation.
C. You have an emotional reaction to the belief.

For example:

A. Your employer falsely accuses you of taking money from her purse and threatens to fire you.
B. You believe, "She has no right to accuse me. She's a bitch!"
C. You feel angry.

If you had held a different belief, your emotional response would have been different:

A. Your employer falsely accuses you of taking money from her purse and threatens to fire you.
B. You believe, "I must not lose my job. That would be unbearable."
C. You feel anxious.

The ABC model shows that **A** does not cause **C**. It is **B** that causes **C**. In the first example, it is not your employer's false accusation and threat that make you angry; it is your belief that she has no right to accuse you, and that she is a bitch. In the second example, it is not her accusation and threat that make you anxious; it is the belief that you must not lose your job, and that losing your job would be unbearable.

---Review---

A variety of examples are given in the hope that all of the readers drawn to our work will understand that many great thinkers of our modern world have spent countless hours, and for some their entire lives, working to create reproducible, duplicable, understandable behavioral models to explain the driving forces behind our actions that promote human evolution.

Shifting Lives has gathered thousands of case files which have lead to our theories pertaining to human behavior. Shifting Lives Method identifies patterns, cyclic behaviors and reaction responses to stimuli [people, places and events] with the use of kinesiology muscle testing and well-crafted questions that are designed to communicate with the subconscious mind.

Shifting Lives Method has brought to light reasonable answers for unexplained actions in human behavior.

The information stored in the subconscious mind is the key to explaining why same or similar upbringings often results in such markedly different outcomes in life patterns.

The subconscious mind chapter will examine the deep underlying, often hidden causes of behavior patterns.

Progress is impossible without change and those who cannot change their minds cannot change anything.

~ George Bernard Shaw ~

Chapter Nine

Subconscious Mind

We are going to move into the subconscious mind.

The subconscious mind creates everything.

We listed it as creating 98% of what you see, so that other two percent can have a variation.

When an ovum and sperm cell come together, they make a cellular division. It divides from two cells and becomes four. It makes one more cellular division. That now becomes eights cells at that point, and is called the neural-streak. That is the beginning of the subconscious mind. So literally two cellular divisions after the sperm and ovum come together, your subconscious mind is being formed at that point.

I like to say that the subconscious mind creates everything, and it does. It creates your body. It is creating everything that your body does. It is taking charge of and running your entire respiratory system. It is taking care of your circulatory system, the heart, all the vessels and all the things that are happening there. It takes care of your digestion.

I want you to picture this for a moment. Think about holding a nice yellow, firm, slightly dimpled object in your hands. We'll call it a lemon.

You take a knife and start cutting through that lemon.

We open up the lemon, and you take half of that lemon and touch it against your lips.

How many of you have some saliva forming in your mouths right now? I'm predicting that a lot of you are reacting to this example as you read these lines.

How does this happen?

All I've said are a couple of words and given a brief example. The subconscious mind takes this information and sends these signals through the amazing cortex part of the brain. The signal goes to the salivary glands that are sitting inside the mouth. The salivary glands create the enzymes necessary to begin to digest a lemon.

Just from a thought.

This is all created from some mysterious part of the brain that has experienced a lemon in the past.

I think that is fascinating.

The subconscious mind is in charge of everything. It is involved in and controls every function of the human body.

The next part of the subconscious that we want to make sure to consider also stores everything. It is taking care of your senses. It is taking care of all of the sights, sounds, tastes, smells and touch. But it is also monitoring the environment outside of just our five normal senses. This portion of the subconscious is recording millions of bits of information every second. We are only aware of a few.

You might be aware of the light around you. You might hear your television set on in the background. Your subconscious mind is monitoring millions of items every single second of every single day.

It not only knows your heart is beating, but it is telling it how to beat, when to beat, and even what the pulse rhythm of that beat is. Signals are sent to a regulating device called the SA node that monitors the heartbeat. But way before that signal is sent to the heart, it has numerous other systems that are telling it exactly what to do. Every second. Every instant. 24-7-365.

The subconscious mind is ruling everything that is going on with the physical body on every level.

Back in the 1880s, a man came along named Sigmund Freud. One thing that he understood well was the subconscious. He knew that the subconscious was in charge of everything, and it was causing situations to occur in people's behavior.

Freud also worked with several other authorities (mentioned in chapter 8) at the time. They knew if they could gain access into the subconscious mind, they could begin changing the way people think, and the way they feel, the things that trouble people in their lives. These experts used an exact formula to speak to and interact with the hidden aspects of the subconscious mind.

The founders of Unity Church, Charles and Myrtle Fillmore were aware of the power of the subconscious mind, what it does, how it acts, how it functions, what it is doing to our world, and how we can communicate with it.

They came up with this beautiful concept using affirmations and prayers. It is a huge part of what Unity Church is today. The use of the daily word, the prayers and affirmations are trying to speak to the subconscious from the outside in. The part that the Fillmores weren't taking into account was that we already have volumes of information in the subconscious mind, creating our daily lives.

The subconscious is a powerful creative force that can very quickly tell a new concept, or idea, "No." Affirmations are one of the most popular tools in use today.

Affirmations are wonderful. We use them in our work. I highly encourage people to use affirmations daily.

But here is one part that falls short when we are using an affirmation; if you are standing in front of a mirror, saying "I am beautiful," and the subconscious mind is saying, "No, you are not," that's the end of that thought, that's the end of that idea. Like the seed planted in sandy soil the new idea cannot take root.

You could say it a hundred thousand times. You could say it a hundred thousand times a day, but the information that is stored inside the subconscious mind is more powerful than something you are trying to introduce from the outside. So the answer is to release and let go of the negative thoughts that are stored in the subconscious mind.

The subconscious stores everything. However you see the world, your experience is shaped through filters in the subconscious mind. I'm going to give you just a quick example.

Let's say you wake up one morning, and have difficulty breathing. And you say to yourself, "Maybe I'll go get checked out, I'll go to a doctor."

You choose to go to a pulmonologist; pulmonologists work on your lungs. You've had trouble breathing, so this decision makes sense. Everything that he's going to do will have some direct focus pertaining to the lungs. Maybe he'll check your lungs' abilities to intake oxygen? He's going to look at the function of the organ, and check tissues around the lung. And he'll examine you based on what he knows, the way a pulmonologist would.

Then you think, "Well, why don't I go to a cardiologist? Maybe the heart is just not beating properly?"

So you go to a good cardiologist. He is most likely going to put you through a stress test. He is going to put you examine the heart function, and might perform some blood work. But his point of view will be based on his training in cardiology.

Let's say you decide to go to a chiropractor. The chiropractor is going to look at you, and he's going to say, "Well, let me see how your spinal segments are doing and your musculature. Maybe I will adjust that certain area of the spine? That will open up that energy that flows to your lungs, heart and circulatory system and will help you out."

The common factor here is that each of these professionals, well trained in what they do, will look at your condition through their unique set of filters.

Earlier we talked about the little brown dog that bites you on the ankle and then later in life you get to make choices: Am I afraid of dogs? Am I afraid of brown dogs? Am I afraid of anything that runs up toward me? That is your set of filters you've created, that's information you are seeing from gathering the information that is in the subconscious mind. There is also some cellular memory that gets involved in these experiences. So we perceive the world through our own unique set of filters.

We can allow our world to run on autopilot. It is your choice. Each of us has a set of experiences that we've gathered over our lifetime. We can now choose what we do with these experiences.

People today allow their world to run on autopilot. They just sit back and let the world come to them and that's okay, its choice. We all can do it. Our body runs on autopilot. As long as were breathing oxygen, eating some food and drinking some water, everything else will just sort of take care of itself.

What is important about this? Do we really want to sit back, and allow the world to just come at us, and then react to it as it unfolds? Or do we want to choose to become more proactive, making choices and decisions about our lives?

We have an opportunity everyday to decide how our days are going to go, what we want to see happen today, and create our world. This is where affirmations come in, and they are wonderful tools. You get up first thing, you are grateful, you are thankful that you are alive and awake. You say some affirmations and get your day started that way. So you are taking charge, making a choice.

Now we're going to digress just a little bit.

We are going to start talking about the brain and the functions of the brain.

Way back when I went to school, the general belief was that the brain was fixed, that you can NOT teach an old dog new tricks. That saying came about because that was the belief of the times. A strong proponent of fixed behavior is B. F. Skinner, with his modeling behaviorism.

Some of the other behavioral psychologists would agree with behaviorism by collecting enough data showing if a child is raised in a certain environment, they can predict the outcome of that child's behavior. Another child raised in a different environment would turn out differently. Therefore if you collect enough data you can say that if the highest percentage of people were raised a certain way, they turn out a certain way. And that proves our point. Modeling is real. Early influences mold our personality, our behavior, and often our socio-economic status.

Today there is now a new way of thinking about the mind. Quantum physics is responsible for bringing a new set of facts to light. Now it is well understood, and mostly agreed upon, that the brain is neuro-plastic. It is not fixed. It is not set in motion by the time you are seven years old. You are not just stuck with it from there on out. You do get to change. You do get to recreate. All the way to the point of the latest, newest, and best data out there, researchers are saying that even in our own genetics changes can be made. Remember the Genetics 2000 Project, where scientists were trying to identify all the genomes and all the different components that make us human? Everything was pretty much mapped and identified. But now geneticists are finding in science, that some of the genetic switches in our body can be turned off or on.

The most interesting thing is how they are turned off and on through our thoughts. It is through our beliefs.

So just because you happen to come out of a family where there is diabetes or cancer or there is something that is a genetically linked disorder, it doesn't mean that you are stuck with that. It doesn't mean that you are set in motion or that this has to happen. There are still choices, and there are ways we can turn off, or turn on these different genetic functions within ourselves. Yes, it is difficult to prove, but possible.

Here is one story about that very subject. The founder of Unity Village, Charles Fillmore, was born in the 1870s. When he was about nine years old, he broke his femur. Back in those days when you broke a major bone like the femur in your leg, you usually died from that injury. Charles survived the broken femur but because of his young age, his body was growing very rapidly.

His healthy leg continued to grow. His wounded leg was stunted in its growth because it was trying to heal. So all of his adult life, his right leg was one inch and a half inches shorter than the left one.

With the use of a built-up sole on his shoe, Charles was able to get around.

In the latter portion of his life, Charles Fillmore began to realize some truly amazing and deep concepts. He understood how the subconscious works.

In the early 1980s, I spent two years at Unity Village, taking courses and studying. There is an archive in the Unity library containing manuscripts that Charles Fillmore wrote that have never been released to the public. His books are a bit difficult to read because he uses his own metaphysical words, then bases his theory on those words, and just assumes you understand.

Charles Fillmore, in the latter years of his life, thought about this leg healing, mending and growing, and by the time of his death, his legs were equal length. He figured out how to tell his subconscious mind how to tell that femur to rebuild itself and grow back to its equal length. That's pretty big news. He discovered something amazing, true and possible. He is a modern day example of the power of the subconscious mind.

There is a concept that people call the Hundredth Monkey. There were these Rochii monkeys that lived on the Okinawa islands during World War II, times when Allied troops were over there blowing up things and destroying the environments of these islands.

The natural food source of these particular monkeys was eliminated. The islanders started bringing in sweet potatoes for these monkeys. At first they would not eat the potatoes because it wasn't their natural food. So they put them aside even though they were starving. But one day, one of the elder monkeys took his sweet potato, and he went to the edge of the water, washed it off, and started eating it. Within just a couple of weeks all of the monkeys started taking the sweet potatoes to the water, scrubbing them off and eating them.

You might say, "Well, so what?"

Well some of those monkeys were on other islands, hundreds of miles away from that first monkey. How did they do it? How did they communicate? How did they know that the monkey over there on another island washed the sweet potato and ate it?

We are all connected. The subconscious mind is connected. All our subconscious minds are connected.

What is keeping the subconscious mind from doing exactly what you want it to do? We'd all like to push a button and make things happen.

There is a scene in the popular movie, The Secret, where a guy sits in a chair. He is moving his right foot, acting like he is shifting gears, and making zoom-zoom noises. The next day, bam, magically he's driving a new sports car.

Many people have tried that, right? Did it work for some of you? It certainly didn't work for all of us. There are reasons why when we give the subconscious mind a new thought or offer a new idea that it doesn't necessarily all of the sudden happen, or happen magically.

The difficult part in an argument is not to defend one's opinion but rather to know it.

~ André' Maurois ~

Chapter Ten

Limiting Factors

I would like to discuss with you Limiting factors.

Control

Control is a major limiting factor on planet earth. We are all bound by certain rules and certain limitations.

An ever-present force like mere gravity is control. Gravity is one of the laws of physics preventing us from just floating around the room. But control in the form of gravity is not something most of us think about every day.

We are controlled by oxygen. Human beings can last about 4 minutes without breathing, and not even very comfortably at that. After about a minute, most of us are squirming around gasping for air.

We can last about 4 days without water, granted, it would not be very comfortable. Even today, we carry around these little plastic bottles, and some of us can't go forty minutes without some water, much less four days. Water is also a source of control.

We are in this physical vessel, stuck here on this planet. Gravity is holding us down. We have to have air. We have to have water. Statistically, we can go for about 40 days without food. But it gets pretty uncomfortable after even four hours. We can't go a long time without these things, because we don't like it and it doesn't feel good.

The other thing that we need is shelter. Our physical body is not set up to deal with extreme heats or extreme colds, so we have to create shelter.

These are all forms of control. Welcome to planet Earth.

When working on people with the Shifting Lives Method, we get deep into the recesses of their subconscious minds and find events. These are often little simple moments, like at age two days, you didn't receive all the food you wanted and it affects your life today in a profound way. This event sets into motion certain fears, doubts, worries, and concerns pertaining to food, meals, and even gatherings where food is the focus.

We've all known someone who can't go five minutes without eating something. They have almonds in their pockets, some bags open, some cookies, something around.

Why is that person like that? Often it's not just choice, it is because of some experience that happened to this person. We like to look at life as one long series of experiences. We lay this life down and sooner or later, we pick up another one. But it's just one more life experience in the subconscious mind. It records everything. It doesn't leave anything out. Edgar Cayce called it "the house of records," and some people give it other names. But somewhere in time and space is this record of everything that has ever happened to you. Everything that you have ever seen, done, touched, heard or experienced is stored in these records. Your subconscious doesn't forget any of it.

I believe the conscious mind is born when we are born, and I believe that the conscious mind dies when we die. That is the frontal lobe portion of the brain. That is where your personality is formed and stored. But that part of us that is timeless is shaped by eons of time, and remembers everything. That timeless element is always there, modifying and controlling your behavior. That is the subconscious mind.

One of the ways that control affects us is in our self worth. Now self worth and self-esteem really are two different things, even though most people join those together.

We place an outward value on our self-esteem. A good example is a certain well-known, high-profile real estate developer/television star, for instance. Everybody knows his name, his brand, his logo, and his prime time reality series. He is famous for naming all of his projects after himself, trumping his competitors with his genius for self-promotion. He would seem to be one of the most confident, high esteem people you could imagine, but from a different point of view, his self worth is actually pretty low.

That is why he has this image he has to project. He has to eat five thousand dollar caviar and have a woman standing beside him who looks a certain way, who measures out dimensionally to be the exact perfect specifications.

Self worth and self-esteem are definitely affected by control. From our Shifting Lives perspective, one of the ways we see control issues present is if the person was raised by a very controlling parent. This upbringing makes you pursue one direction or the other. You either become a very controlling person, or you become a person that is so sheepish and broken down that you have no self-esteem. With this presentation, you aren't going to be controlling because you don't have enough personal power.

Criticism

How did criticism make the list, and why is it here? One of the tools of a controlling person is criticism. Controllers gain their control over someone else by criticizing them. If we think more about this in terms of children, a critical parent is trying to control with criticism, which will certainly affect the self-esteem and self worth of that child.

Let's look at the parent/child relationship. If a parent is rejecting a child, that is going to directly affect self-esteem, and self worth. It makes you feel punished, and it makes you feel unwanted, which leads us directly into abandonment.

Abandonment

Abandonment sounds a lot like rejection but it has its own unique attributes. A lot of people feel abandoned in certain ways, and it could be manifested even from if a parent decides to go somewhere and leaves you at home, leaves you at the sitter's or just leaves you out of the activity, creating this whole abandonment issue.

The feeling of abandoned shows up in our everyday life in the form of lack of trust with all people. Feeling left out of parties and social gatherings is common, even though you really didn't want to attend them anyway.

That is a funny aspect of feeling abandoned. People don't want to be around people they don't trust, yet they feel lonely, hurt and insulted when not asked to attend a party.

It all directly affects our self worth, and our self-esteem.

Self-punishment

A major theme affecting lives is self-punishment. Self-punishment is an interesting dilemma. It is like a prison that we build for ourselves. It is custom made, and constructed by us. It is locked by us, and made for our own amusement. We create this jail cell and place ourselves inside of it because we have accumulated guilt from various constructs.

The simplest event can cause a developing child to heap this guilt onto themselves, creating self-punishment. Let's say that your parents were having a fight one day, and you were sitting nearby as an observer or a witness to it, but you feel like the fight was your fault. You start heaping this guilt onto yourself, but it really has nothing to do with you. You were not involved. Your parents were just fighting because couples fight. But you lock this feeling away, then each time an event similar to this happens, the self-punishment gets deeper and deeper. This is a self-imposed prison that you have created. The door becomes thicker and stronger. The key gets more rusty, and the door becomes more difficult to open than ever before.

This is a very important concept to begin looking at in your own life.

Gossip

One of the things that help us to make this self-imposed prison worse is gossip.

Many of people tend to do it. It's hard to stay away from gossip. It's on everything you see today. If you turn on a television, even for a second, you can't miss the ever-present gossip shows. Everything we look at basically is gossip. It's who did what to whom, who is guilty, whose fault was it, who is going to be the next top model, and do they have to slam on the other people so they can win?

Shows like "Survivor," this is reality drama. We are pinning this person against that person. That is what these shows thrive on, pulling a person aside and saying, "let's talk about them, do you want them in allegiance with you or why do you want them out?" So it's a very real issue. It is a very hard-set core of the basic societal constructs. It is gossip. I would ask you not to do it, and give you some reasons why not.

Judgment

Another limited factor is judgment. Judgment is very powerful. The difference between observation and judgment can be a very fine line.

Often we look at something and think, "Is that an observation or is that a judgment?" Some of these things you really need to ask yourself, and if you find yourself criticizing something or someone more than once or twice in a month or so, you might say that is a judgment.

What are we looking at? What are we judging when we do make a judgment? We are really just looking at ourselves. And we really are just looking at our reflection in the mirror of consciousness.

We think we are seeing some aspect of another person, something that seems or appears to be outside of ourselves that we are assigning to ourselves. Yet we are blaming and pointing the finger, saying it is them, it is that person. They drive too fast. They drive too slow. They drive too big of a vehicle. They drive too small of a vehicle. These types of statements are judgments. Notice your judgments and the things you judge, then make notes in your daily observations. Turn judgment into observation. Use observation to bring about change. Awareness is the first step towards healing.

Negative Thoughts

Negative thoughts are huge. We all have them. They arise, but it is what you do with them that becomes important. Do you let the thought come out and manifest itself, or do you stop it right where it is? As soon as you have a negative thought, there's technique after technique to help you just stop it right there and not let it grow, fester and manifest into a horrible crisis. Refrain from speaking negative words. Take control of the reactive mind. Become proactive.

Think before you speak.

Anger

Have you ever been in a situation where anger breaks out in a room? It might start with just one person, then it becomes a tidal wave which drags you into it. Anger seems to create itself, manifesting from nowhere.

Anger is one of those energies that can very quickly overpower and overtake people. A lot of its power is physiological. There are certain things that happen when anger erupts in a room, and you've experienced it. We've all seen it. Consider in the olden days when the townspeople used to track down a bank robber and then have a lynching in the square. All of the town's citizens come out of their homes to watch this guy get hung up by a rope. They are all yelling, screaming, "He did it. He's the one. He's the bad guy. Hang him!"

It is this scapegoat-type theory that fuels the madness of anger.

Back in New Testament times, there was this occurrence where a woman was caught in the act of adultery. The law at the time was for the villagers to pick up stones and stone this woman to death. We've moved away from that a little bit in our more modern world, but as the story goes there was this wise man there. He looked at each one of these villagers holding stones and looked at this woman, saying, "He among you who is without sin, cast the first stone." And then he went about his business for a moment. When he looked up at the woman he said, "Woman, where have your accusers gone?" She said that they had all gone away. He then said, "Well neither do I accuse you."

Now, why is that important? Why is that more than some little story that took only a couple of lines in a scripture from a couple thousand years ago?

First off, the woman was caught in the very act of adultery. There was no question of it happening. There was no one saying, "I think she did it." She was caught in the act. It makes sense that they would be that specific. Then these villagers show up to do what was the tradition of the time, throw these big stones and pummel this woman to death. Yet this wise man comes and says to these people, "If you are without sin yourself, go ahead and do it." And obviously no one could cast the first stone, because we all have our shortcomings.

The very important part about this is that he just simply said, "Neither do I render judgment against you."

 I would ask you to look at your life, notice the things in your world that you tend to observe and turn into judgment. If you find things that bug you, write them down. Then take a look at them. Why is it that really strange people bother you? Why is it that someone that has things all over their body bothers you? I know you have something that bothers you. It might be relatives, short people, fat people, people with hair, people without hair. If something bothers you, just make a note of it.

Examine it and ask yourself why it bothers you, because chances are anything you are making a judgment about, you've been that.

There's a speaker on the circuit today that I really admire. His name is Gregg Braden. He is interested in the ancient traditions, similar to the work that Joseph Campbell is best known for. Joseph went all around the world, exploring every nook and cranny of the planet. He studied the traditions that people lived by. He explored the most ancient cultures. Joseph Campbell was famous for finding the similarities among culture. He wasn't looking for the differences. He may have started out looking for the differences, but he became wiser over the years, realizing how the aborigines in Australia and the native American Indians had very similar beliefs about a bird in the sky that was the fire god. And you know people in the Middle East believe certain things that people over here believe. And he brought all of these traditions together, finding amazing similarities among all of the people of all nations in every corner of the globe.

Gregg Braden took that type of work and studied it. He studied the Peruvians and ancient people, particularly the Native Americans. He found these amazing traditions and similarities in people. But here is one of the things he brought to mind that I've really focused on: we have all been victims. I'm not necessarily just talking about in this lifetime. Likewise, we have all been the oppressor. And here's the third part: we've all been witness to horrific, life-changing events.

Consider our earlier example of the now infamous brown dog. We started with the brown dog coming up and biting you. Then you began to make choices as to how you were going to react to that experience. You could have just been the witness to that scene.

We've all been prisoners of war, and we've all been guards controlling the prisoners. We have all been witnesses to those events. We've all been the posse that goes after that bank robber. We have all observed the lynching. We've played all of those roles.

If this is a difficult concept for you to grasp, just look at it through the filters that you already have in place. How is it that one child is born and by age 3 can play Beethoven and Bach, and never had a piano lesson? How does a child come out of the womb, then create amazing paintings, and never had a lesson?

Or take the opposite of these examples, a child is born with a cleft palate or some life-altering birth defect, reducing the changes of ever having a normal life.

So if anywhere in your brain is the belief of a God who doles out fairness and wonderful, creative, joyous gifts, just think about it for a minute. If that is true, then life is not very fair. And that type of thinking is placing a human emotion, a human attribute onto something that is far more amazing than anything I'll even attempt to describe. Because whatever created, not only this planet but the solar system, not only the solar system but the universe, not only this universe but all other universes known or unknown is beyond description with our human language.

Consider the possibility that we live one big long life. Perhaps we pop in and out of different forms and different shapes, and we've all had numerous life experiences?

"Give me a dozen healthy infants, well-formed, and my own specified world to bring them up in and I'll guarantee to take any one at random and train him to become any type of specialist. I might select — doctor, lawyer, artist, merchant-chief and, yes, even beggar-man and thief, regardless of his talents, penchants, tendencies, abilities, vocations, and race of his ancestors. I am going beyond my facts and I admit it, but so have the advocates of the contrary and they have been doing it for many thousands of years." [Behaviorism (1930), p. 82]

~ John B Watson ~

Chapter Eleven

The Solution

I believe inside each of you there is a musician, artist, or some amazing performer who has something to contribute to life.

The solution is to release your fears, doubts, worries and negative beliefs from your subconscious mind. If you release your fears from the subconscious mind, it opens up amazing possibilities for your life. When you release doubts, worries, judgments and guilt from the subconscious mind, it opens up even greater possibilities. It is like opening up the jail cell door and letting yourself out.

So what are some of the types of things we can do, to get rid of these beliefs?

Previously, we talked a little bit about affirmations. We've talked briefly about different technologies, methods, and practices which many disciplines teach, claiming to release negative experiences.

We have talked about rewriting the story of your past, stating that rewriting is one of the techniques that you can use. You literally can do that. You can go back and rewrite the past that you remember. I'm not talking about changing your childhood, where you went to high school, or changing your parents. I'm talking about changing the perspective through which you see your parents, schools, friends and the experiences that you were involved in during your past.

Maybe a brown dog came up and bit you, and you get the opportunity to go back and say "huh, well maybe brown dogs aren't so bad after all."

I would like to introduce a new concept that I call "X Marks the Spot."

I'm going to make a suggestion: today, right now: put a big X on a piece of paper.

From this moment forward you get to make a new choice. You get to decide whether you want to continue your story the way it is, the way it has been written, the way you perceive your life, or do you want to rewrite your stories starting from this exact moment and moving forward?

You have the chance to look closely at your life, consider your situation, notice your circumstances and see them from a new prospective. Choose now to end your pain and suffering.

It's about choice. Your choice! Choose Now!

Albert Einstein said, "You cannot solve a problem with the same mind that created it." What did he mean? He meant that you can't work yourself out of a situation with the same mindset that put you there. I'm not talking about external things, like the debate over global warming. That's not exactly what we're concerned about. We're concerned about where you are in your life, where you want to be with relationships, career and finances. How do you make your world different/ better?

You recreate, and you restructure your life. You take what you know now and you move forward with it. You remember this book. Dr. Keith is saying don't judge people, places or events. Think about it before you gossip. Think about the certain criteria you want to live by, and you can restructure that portion of your life. Stop allowing yourself to get into a negative way of thinking. Even if it's the very smallest thing, even if it's getting perturbed about the cashier that took fourteen seconds too long to scan items into the register. Stop negative thoughts from large scale events down to the smallest occurrence. Let this be true in all of your life situations.

We started Chapter 7 of this book by saying that you are many component parts. You are a system of various moving parts, and every part is important to the whole. Think about that for a moment. Ponder this section of the book until you develop a deep sense of understanding related to the complexity of your human experience.

Notice What You're Noticing.

We said cellular memory is an important part of this equation. We all carry memories within our cell structure. It's in our DNA. It's in our structure. It's in that special something that makes us human beings.

There are also archetypal energies stored in the mind. Jung popularized them, and Caroline Myss has taken his work and really gone into depth with it, talking about all of the archetypes, such as the victim, the wounded child, and all aspects of magical thinking. Both Jung and Myss have popularized these ideas, and these concepts have an effect on our daily lives. Like the stages of personal development, we shift in and out of archetypes depending on the circumstances.

But here's the question I would like for you to ask yourself. Can you withstand the destruction caused by a negative thought? I crafted this question from a book that I once read about the dangerous effects of negative thinking. I restructured the phrase to suit this idea. If we all truly knew how our thinking profoundly affected our lives, and our health, maybe we would pay closer attention to our every thought.

How then can we eliminate negative thoughts?

The following are the beginning steps: love and accept ourselves, develop compassion for others, find understanding for other people's points of view, and move yourself into a place of allowance and acceptance.

How then do we do accomplish this new perspective?

Gather your own opinion based on personal experience. Seek your own knowledge through research. You don't truly know a man until you have walked a mile in his shoes. Stop criticizing the outward appearance of people, places or events. This helps to reduce judgments, remembering that there are three sides to every story. I won't bore you with the details because we've all been the victim, we've all been the witness, and we've all been the aggressor.

Judgment is one source of negative thinking. How do you release judgments? First you observe your life and note where you are making your judgments, then move yourself up in state by shifting yourself out of the second and third order of thinking. (See Chapter 8.)

People! We are not static thinkers. Let's make that perfectly clear.

In the personal behavioral stages discussed earlier, unfortunately we are not all in the fifth order. We can be when we are in a certain meditative state where everything is perfect. Then you come out of that state when you leave the meditation.

Throughout the course of our daily activities, we move in and out of these stages, so the key here is to notice when you slide back into second order thinking and begin saying "those people are a barrier to me getting what I want, and I don't like it. I'm going to blow them up or kill them."

So watch yourself, watch when you move in and out of these stages, and work diligently to keep yourself in a loving place.

You can best accomplish this higher state by noticing the similarities in people rather than the differences. Always ask yourself, "Am I noticing the similarities in the people that I just criticized or demonized?"

How do we accelerate our own personal growth? The following are popular methods used today.

Acquiring knowledge from books, that's what we do right? We all read books. You say to yourself, "If I can just read one more book, I'm sure I'll find the answer."

You think, "the book that I am currently reading told me to read this new book, and I'll get what I'm looking for if I read that book, but I get to the end chapter and I didn't find it."

Even the big books that some of us read, two thousand something pages long, is the answer there? Well it might be, but hopefully we don't miss the exact page where the secret is written.

DVDS are popular today. Everyone seems to be making "The Secret," "Beyond the Secret", "The Other Side of the Secret", "The Secret to the Secret," and on and on.

Is the answer to be found in that? No.

The answer is within you, hidden in your own subconscious mind. It is that action center that makes things happen. How then do we access the answer? Meditation is a great practice. I highly recommend it. Find a way, find a style that fits your physical abilities, and develop something that works for you. Breathing exercises are also a wonderful way to relax and clear the mind. The body's first memory outside of the womb is the breath. Many practices center around breathing.

Affirmations are also quite good. There are many styles, and numerous techniques. I recommend that you say them daily. Twice each day is even better. I encourage it. Hopefully, you will gain an appreciation for them and make your affirmations very detailed and very specific. Don't just get up in the morning and say that you want to be rich. Be specific. State that you want to make forty thousand dollars a month. I want it to come in this form: I am willing to provide this service in exchange for this money. I am at least willing to walk out into the front yard and pick it up when it falls out of the sky. Make your affirmation very detailed and specific. Perhaps you have wanted to go back to school? What is this school? What is it that you want to study? Where do you want to go? What hours do you want to participate? Do you want to go full time or part time? What do you want to learn? Speak your affirmations out loud with emotion.

You may say that you want a new man in your life. Well how tall is he? What does he look like? What does he do? Where is he from? What qualities do you want him to have? What kind of background does he have? Each of these details is important.

Be specific and **write it down**! I don't believe that whoever or whatever created this world was just like, "Ohhh, I think I'll make a world today." No. I believe that very specific descriptions were spoken.

Removing the old tapes and the limiting beliefs from the subconscious mind is the quickest way to achieve success. You can get the trash that's stored in the subconscious mind out. You can rewrite your past, and clear your subconscious.

There are methods and techniques to make these things happen for you. There are various schools of thought; philosophers and great thinkers have been working on this concept for eons of time. How do we release our fears? How do we release our doubts? Our concerns? Our judgments? These constructs are trapped inside the subconscious mind, and there is a way to identify them and release them.

Let's review:

1) Release judgments, guilt, fear, anger and self punishment

2) Find the similarity in people, places and events

3) Love yourself, others and your creator with all of your being

4) Become your own best observer, monitor every thought

5) Pursue diligently acceptance, appreciation and balance.

Shifting Lives Method

We have finally arrived at the place where Deborah and I can share with you our method. We use muscle testing to ask your subconscious mind questions. Though muscle testing may appear simple to the observer, there is skill required to receive accurate answers. Your muscles and brain are hard-wired to answer yes and no questions.

In the Old Testament there were several references to the Urim and Thummin, stones used to represent light and perfection, yes or no. The priests at the time were given yes or no answers by casting or throwing these objects. The priests used this method to speak to God.

We are created in a fashion that allows this yes or no, true or false questioning to answer life's deep secrets. Muscle testing works on the same principle: yes and no. The key is well-structured questions. These questions are the heart of the fact-finding portion of our work.

Remember: It's Not Them.

Deep exploration into your subconscious mind reveals people, places and events that have been deeply etched by experiences and stored as memories in the subconscious.

Shifting Lives has developed a method of exploration that probes into the recesses of the storage centers we call the subconscious mind. With the use of muscle testing, informative answers are obtained to the otherwise unanswered questions left unspoken about our repressed experiences. We have developed a strategic type of properly stated questions, speaking the language that the subconscious responds to, unlike forms of hypnosis and other system.

Shifting Lives Method has found the key to unlock the mystery of the mind. This method cuts through years of conventional talk therapy, accelerating your growth by decades. Each unique event has created your individual life experience and can be accessed with lightning speed and laser precision.

Who can benefit from Shifting Lives Method?

Shifting Lives Method helps everybody. From lonely singles who want to meet the love of their life, to the high-powered business executive who has made the wrong business decision again and again, to the aspiring artists out there trying to make a name for themselves, all are helped by Shifting Lives Method. Athletes, performers and artists that are at the top of their careers, looking to take it to the next level, will benefit from our work. We have already worked with many world-class athletes, top of the chart bands and multimillionaire entrepreneurs, seeing tangible results.

The real intent and focus of this work is to not only offer an explanation for personal behavior, but to offer a solution as well. This solution is obtainable by all people, not just the privileged few. Our goal at Shifting Lives is to provide a workable solution to patterns of fear, guilt, self-doubt, relationship and financial issues.

Shifting Lives makes an open call to everyone who would like to move up to the next level. We are available to help World Champion Golfers, Cyclists, Professional Racecar Drivers, Musicians, Actors and of course, all people of all kinds at all levels of development who desire to shift their lives. Whether you are a schoolteacher or an accountant, a craftsperson or a marketing executive, a mother or a father, a senior citizen or a twenty-something, Shifting Lives offers benefits for each and every one of you.

Find out how amazing your life can be without fear, guilt, judgments and conflicts between your conscious and subconscious mind. You can learn the Shifting Lives Method by visiting shiftinglives.com.

Daily Practices

- ❖ Gratitude – Upon wakening each and every morning, give gratitude by stating aloud "gratitude" for your physical body, your home and possessions, and your relationships. Also practicing this each night just before falling asleep is recommended.

- ❖ Affirmations – Hand write your favorite affirmations on the topics most important to you at the moment. Speak these positive statements aloud, affirming with strong feeling. Remember, when stating personal affirmations looking into a mirror adds power.

- ❖ Meditation – Use a method and posture that works well with your physical body. The key to success with meditation is consistency.

- ❖ Breathing – Being aware of and noticing the breath is the beginning. There are several popular methods. Choose the one you are most comfortable with, and then do it.

- ❖ Yoga, Chi Gong and walking – Especially when practiced outdoors, both are amazing for your physical well being and calmness of mind.

- ❖ Read and begin to surround yourself with positive words, thoughts, books, and phrases.

❖ Listen to positive CDs – as often as possible. There are some that contain subliminal affirmations.

❖ Wallpaper your computer screen with positive images or affirmations.

❖ Journaling – Writing your thoughts first thing upon awakening has proven to be most powerful. Consistency is the key.

❖ Visualization – Create a vision board with your fondest desires, such as your favorite home or relationship. Visualizing positive images morning and evening.

❖ Conscious intentions for the day, best practiced immediately upon awakening. Be detailed, clear and concise with your stated intentions. Begin watching for confirmations.

❖ Practice positive relationships with everyone you come in contact with and notice what you are noticing.

❖ Observe – Find the similarities in people, places and events. Notice what you are noticing.

❖ Allow – Accept – Appreciate.

❖ Speak love and healing to others.

❖ Isn't it interesting that I feel this way? Let this become a statement whenever you feel physical pain or anxiety in any situation.

Affirmations

I create abundance in all I say and do.
I attract positive minded people.

I choose love, joy and freedom.
I have an open heart filled with love.
All my relationships are loving and harmonious.
My life is filled with love, fun & happiness.
I am healthy, whole and fit.
I think positive thoughts.

I love myself.
I believe in myself.
I trust myself.

I give and express love easily.
I am happy and peaceful.
I am loved and accepted by everyone.
I am safe and I am loved.
God loves me just the way I am.

My physical body is perfect.
My body is healthy, whole and fit.

I prosper others and they prosper me.
I am living an abundantly prosperous life.
I am worthy to be wealthy.
I am supported by the universe to be prosperous.

My job is peaceful and happy.
Everyone I work with is kind & loving.
I love and enjoy the work I do every day.
I am making _______ amount of money every
week/month.
The power of God is working with me to make my
dreams come true.

Knowing our words are powerful we feel & see the
reality of our positive spoken words.
We focus positive energy and speak positive words.
Everything I desire comes to me quickly and easily.
Every movement I make, every action I take, every
thought that I create is for the greater good.

I open wide the window of my mind allowing access to
new ideas and concepts.

God has given me all of the riches of heaven and I
bless others with my gifts.

I was created to be an expression of love and
prosperity. Shalom to all aspects of myself.

God leads me into the path of peace and tranquility.

There is no limit to the gifts I receive from my creator.

Everything I put my hands to is blessed.

I wish for all men love, emotional health and
prosperity.

Forgiveness Prayer

______________I forgive you for anything and everything that you have ever done to me.

Thank you for forgiving me for anything and everything that I have ever done to you.

I release and let go of any and all <u>emotions</u> associated with our relationship.

Recommended use of this prayer

First, state the name of the person that you have selected to seek forgiveness from. Speak this prayer out loud. Say it with as much conviction as you possibly can, even if it is painful. Speak this prayer repeatedly, several times a day. It is best if you can speak it out every time you think of the person, even if it is hundreds of times a day for several weeks. Depending on the severity of the perceived offense, this technique may take weeks of persistent repetition. Continue to use this prayer until you truly feel peace, ease and balance toward yourself and the person chosen to release.

In extreme cases anger, fear, disgust, even rage may arise. If this occurs, state the specific emotion in the prayer in place of the word emotions. My personal experience with this prayer leads me to believe that staying with the first person chosen to forgive until all of the negative feelings are balanced is best. Use this prayer for anyone and everyone that you have ever had interactions with, even if you do not necessarily feel a negative interaction has occurred. Last, but not least, perform this prayer for yourself. State your name and forgive yourself for everything that you have ever done to yourself. Looking at yourself in a mirror further empowers the message.

A Note About The Authors

Dr. Keith South was born in Long Beach, CA and raised in Memphis, TN. He graduated from Cleveland College with a Bachelor of Science in Human Biology, and he further advanced his education at the Cleveland Chiropractic College where he obtained his Doctorate of Chiropractic.

Dr. South has been studying and practicing Acupuncture for 33 years and is a certified Acupuncturist. In addition to his 15 years of Chiropractic experience, Dr. South has more than 38 years experience in the practice and instruction of Martial Arts and has special training in the fields of Kinesiology and Herbology.

To date Dr South has counseled more than four thousand clients using the Shifting Lives Method. His motivational speeches have inspired thousands.

Dr South has coached CEOs, professional athletes, songwriters, performers, and some of the world's best known speakers. He is dedicated to the improvement and enhancement of life for everyone, and is diligent in using the most natural means possible.

Deborah A. South D.D. is a gifted natural healer. At a very young age she demonstrated the ability to look deep within a person's psyche.

Deborah has dedicated her life to the study of Herbology, nutrition, and the art of healing. She is, and always has been, deeply spiritual, experiencing many of the world's most revered spiritual paths. Through her guidance hundreds of people have experienced profound physical and psychological healing.

She is a true believer in the self-realization journey and Christ consciousness. A co-founder in the technique now known as Shifting Lives Method.

Deborah's deepest desire is to share this amazing life transforming work with as many people as is humanly possible.

Shifting Lives Institute offers:

Personal Sessions

Facilitator Training

Certified Facilitator Training

Dr South is available for speaking engagements, workshops, and corporate training.

Recommended Reading

Bailes, Frederick, *Your Mind Can Heal You*

Braden, Gregg, *Divine Matrix*

Campbell, Joseph, *The Way of Animal Powers*

Castle, Victoria, *The Trance of Scarcity*

Dyer, Wayne, *Wisdom of the Ages*

Ellis, Albert, *How to Stubbornly Refuse to Make Yourself Miserable About Anything Yes Anything.*

Fillmore, Charles, *12 Powers of Man*

Hall, Calvin, *A Primer of Freudian Psychology*

Hawkins, David, *Truth Versus Falsehood*

Keen, Sam, *The Passionate Life*

Klotz-Douglass Neal, *Prayers of the Cosmos*

Lewis, Spencer, *Self-mastery & Fate, with the Cycles of Life*

Maslow, Abraham, *Toward a Psychology of Being*

Merton, Thomas, *No Man is Island*

Millman, Dan, *The Warrior Athlete*

Murphy, Joseph, *Peace Within Yourself*

Murphy, Joseph, *The Power of the Subconscious Mind*

Myss, Caroline, *Sacred Contracts*

Smith, Philip, *Total Breathing*

Talbot, Michael, *The Holographic Universe*

Truman, Karol, *Feelings Buried Alive Never Die*

Wilber, Ken, *A Brief History of Everything*

Vibrational Formulas

These herbal/vitamin proprietary formulas are created to balance specific emotional issues working to release them to bring change in a specific area of one's life.

They are based on frequency and energetic knowledge shifting you to a position of empowerment, placing you back in control of your life.

The ingredients in each formula are synergistic, releasing negative cellular memory, balancing your energy and shifting you to a place of empowerment.

Available at Shiftinglives.com

Formula #1 **The Home Formula.** Promotes feeling comfortable in your physical body. Subconsciously 99.9% of people tested are not happy in their bodies. The focus being on abandonment by our creator because we can't see the creator right now. This formula allows you to accept yourself & connect to your higher spiritual resources.

Formula #2 **Love for Baby.** Many emotions settle in the ovaries. This formula supports the reproductive organs for women wanting a baby. This formula releases unloved, disgust, fear of pregnancy, lack of emotions and worry. This is also helpful with guilt & shame in the physical act of love making.

Formula #3 **The Working Formula.** Take control of your career, job, work. This formula also targets low self-esteem. Every person on earth has some type of issue with their self-esteem. You can improve your self worth allowing you to receive good things in life making the path much clearer.

Formula #4 **The Clarity Formula.** This formula releases the negative energy which settles in the Thyroid area showing in the form of, muddled thinking, paranoia, emotional instability, up & down. It also helps with over concern for others & lack of control over events.

Formula #5 **The Purifier of Relationships.** Our testing shows that 99.9% of people are not able to give and/or receive love. The ability to love has been impeded by being unloved resulting in low self-esteem. This formula may help bring in the love of your life or your soul mate. It is effective on any one that you have a personal relationship with.

Formula #6 **The Personality Shifter**. Our personalities are affected by our low self-esteem and our loss of personal power. Many of us have no personal power whatsoever which may show in a lack of energy or being tired all the time.

Formula #7 **The Forgiving One.** Often we have hidden resentment & unforgiveness for people and experiences we have forgotten or blocked from our memory. This formula helps release trapped resentment in the Gallbladder. It also helps with unforgiveness, allowing you to have stronger faith & connect to higher spiritual resources while strengthening your communication with God and his angelic host.

Formula #8 **The Poverty/Greed Formula.** This formula brings a shift in financial issues and releases the cellular memory of poverty. Effective in releasing the negative constructs about money. Money is an energy exchange and by releasing the desire to control will benefit us greatly leading us to prosperity and peace.

Formula #1 $29.99
Formula #2 $44.99
Formula #3 $26.99
Formula #4 $29.99
Formula #5 $28.99
Formula #6 $29.99
Formula #7 $34.99
Formula #8 $34.99

Prices are subject to change.

Available at Shiftinglives.com

LaVergne, TN USA
03 January 2011
210940LV00001BA/50/P